HOW TO SUCCEED AS A
MALE MODEL
BY ERIC PERKINS

HOW TO SUCCEED AS A
MALE MODEL
BY ERIC PERKINS

Nautilus Books, Inc
New York

Nautilus Books, Inc.
496 LaGuardia Place
Suite 145
New York, NY 10012

Library of Congress Cataloging-in-Publication Data

Perkins, Eric.
    How to succeed as a male model / by Eric Perkins. -- 1st ed.
        p.   cm.
    Includes index.
    ISBN 0-935055-40-1 (pbk. : alk. paper) : $12.95
    1. Models, Fashion--Vocational guidance. 2. Employment of men.
I. Title
HD8039.M77P47   1989
659.1'52--dc19   88-38564
                                                                      CIP

PRINTED ON ACID-FREE PAPER

Printed in the United States of America

10 9 8 7 6 5 4 3 2 1

First Edition

This book is dedicated to the gang.

CONTENTS

SECTION TWO: MODEL INTERVIEWS

SECTION THREE: RESOURCES

ACKNOWLEDGMENTS

There are many people who helped make this book a reality. I wish to thank them all.

Sean Byrnes
Kathy Daab
Gloria Dare
HV Models
Christopher Ottaunick
Francesco Scavullo
Wilhelmina Models
Zoli Models

Special thanks to all the models who found the time to be interviewed for this book.

Kyle Cody
Darren Coté
Cody Cupper
Michael Dupre
John Enos
Bill Gordon
Jesse Harris
Carl Holmes
Chris John

Stan Newman
Campion Platt
Rob Simonson
Brian Solano
Tom Tripodi
A. J. Vincent
Renauld White
Jason Workman

Cover photograph of John Enos
Styled by Sean M. Byrnes
Photographed by Francesco Scavullo

INTRODUCTION

Not so many years ago, a guy considering a career in modeling would have been laughed at. Now, a lot of those male models are laughing all the way to the bank. Male modeling has exploded in the last few years, becoming not only respectable, but a hot commodity as well.

Guys who were in college studying to become doctors, lawyers, and engineers are dropping out to earn some fast bucks in front of the camera. Many of them are doing so well that it's unlikely that they will ever go back. Today it's possible for a male model to make up to $4,000 for a day's work, and even much more with bonuses and usuage fees added on. At this rate, they are beginning to give female models some real competition, who have traditionally always made much more money than the men.

Now it's not at all unusual to see men hitting the runways of the world modeling the latest fashions from Paris or Milan and causing a sensation. All the top fashion magazines are overflowing with male models perfectly at home in front of the cameras of the world's top photographers. It may be Paris one day, London the next, and Tokyo the day after. The world is becoming their oyster.

If little girls are dreaming of growing up to become the next Paulina or Christie Brinkley, then little boys are dreaming of becoming the next Tom Selleck or Ted Danson, who both began their careers as models. In fact, a male model is likely to have a much longer career than a female model if he cares to stick with it. Most women can only model until their mid twenties, but a male model can easily continue on into his fifties or beyond if he is so inclined.

But before you get the idea that modeling is a great way to get rich quick, bear in mind that it's a very specialized field of endeavor, and not just anyone is right for it. Before you hit the Big Bucks Bonanza, there are likely to be a few years of near starvation, hard knocks and rejection in abundance. There are plenty of men out there who want to be male models every bit as much as you do, or more, which makes the competition hot and heavy. There's always a story of a guy being discovered on the beach and the next month he's on the cover of GQ, but don't count on it. That happens only very rarely. There's more to the business than just good timing. You must have the correct physical attributes, the right "look", and a terrific personality if you expect to make it big.

In the chapters that follow, you'll learn just what the qualifications are, and how to break into this exciting field *and survive.* All the information that you need to begin a successful career is right here in these pages, so read on!

SECTION ONE

THE BASICS

CHAPTER ONE

START WITH THE BASICS

If you would like to make modeling a part of your future, you must learn the requirements of the profession. These requirements vary according to the location you are in, and the local opportunities. Top models, or those who are able to make a good living at modeling on a full-time basis, are usually only found in the very large cities of the world. Smaller cities may have many opportunities, but the smaller the city, the less work there is likely to be.

The top city in the world for male models is New York City. New York pays top dollar for everything, and probably has more advertising work booked from there than any other city in the world, and advertising is where the money is. For editorial (magazine work) a male model almost has to visit Europe. There is much more editorial work available there than in the U.S. and many new models start there to build up their portfolios. Editorial work pays far less than advertising work, but the tearsheets from these bookings enable a model to get advertising bookings.

In New York and Europe there are certain standards that a male model must live up to. Although these requirements are not completely rigid, they must be fairly closely adhered to if you expect big success.

First of all there is a height requirement. You should be a minimum of six feet tall and a maximum of six-two. Your ideal suit size should be a 40 regular, although some models can get away with as much as a 42 long, you should be very good looking and in top physical shape. You are, of course, expected to show up on time and be ready and willing to work, with a positive attitude.

Beyond that come the intangibles. You must be photogenic and possess a certain quality of energy and excitement that comes across whether you are on a runway or in front of a camera. Your personality must be exceptional, keeping those around you in an "up" frame of mind, and caught up in your excitement.

If you think you fit these requirements, then there's a possibility of a successful career ahead of you. But remember, not every top model has all of the requirements listed above. There are always compensating factors. If a man is extremely good looking, he might get away with being only five foot eleven or six foot three. An inch one way or the other may not make a big difference if you have some other attribute that is exceptional. However, bear in mind that the more unusual you are, the less likely that you will have a long successful career.

For those people who really do not fit the requirements above and are not exceptional, there is always the possibility of working in a different market. All cities are not so particular, and not all jobs are right for the "fashion model" type. Guys who are only five foot ten but fit other requirements might get lots of work in Los Angeles or Chicago, and if they can act they can do commercials, where there are no height requirements at all, generally speaking. We will discuss some of the markets for those of you who don't fit the requirements of a fashion model in a later chapter.

Beyond the physical attributes and the "intangibles", there is still the business of getting *into* the business. This can take many forms. It's true that you may be discovered on the beach or on a college campus, but there are basically two ways of being "discovered." One way is to have the modeling agencies come to you, the other way is for you to go to them. Modeling agents *will* come to you under the right set of circumstances. Agents do a fair amount of scouting to find their models, and as a result, you will find a great many of them at modeling conventions that are held regularly in many different parts of the United States and Canada. These conventions are usually attended by students of modeling schools, and it may be impossible to attend if you are not with a school. These conventions are expensive, often costing between one and two thousand dollars to attend, but as many agents are in attendance, this can be a good deal if you are discovered. More about conventions and modeling schools will be discussed in a later chapter.

Making the rounds of the modeling agencies is the best way to find out if you've got what it takes. While the top agencies are in the big cities, it will do you no harm to start right in your home town. You may think that a home town agency will do you no good if New York is your destination, but there you would most probably be wrong. A local agency may find you some part time work in the business, and give you some exposure. It's the perfect time to start developing your technique in front of the camera and on the runway, and becoming experienced and comfortable. A bonus is that most small agencies are connected in some way with a larger one in a larger city. If they feel you have potential, they may recommend you to a larger agency that can get you bigger and better work. Most model scouts from the big New York agencies are in contact with smaller agencies all across the United States on a regular basis.

If you decide to come directly to New York, and hundreds of young models do, you will need some photographs to show. This is very important, as agents are not only interested in what you look like, but also how well you photograph. *A portfolio is not required in the beginning.* This is emphasized because a lot of young people will spent hundreds or thousands of dollars on "professional" pictures that they don't need, and agents are appalled to see. A few simple snapshots are all that is necessary. These photos should show you clearly, but even Polaroids will do.

Before you can get much work, a portfolio will be necessary. A beginning portfolio is usually made up from test shootings. Test shootings are done for the benefit of everyone's portfolio; the photographer's, model's, stylist, hair & makeup, etc. Everyone usually works for free, or charges a minimum to cover expenses only. A photographer might charge the model for film and processing. If a greater fee is involved, then the photographer is likely making money on the deal, and this should not rightly be called a test, but a paid assignment. Since there are almost always photographers who will do genuine testing, it is best to seek out these people, who are often just starting themselves, and are likely to have fresh and exciting ideas.

Your agency will help you put together your portfolio, and will send you out on go-sees when they feel you are ready. Any photographs that are the result of your jobs will be incorporated into your portfolio if your agent feels that they are good photos. Eventually, over a period of many months (or more), all of your tests should be replaced with actual tearsheets from jobs that you have done. You will always be updating you portfolio; new tearsheets will always be replacing old ones.

Before we get off the subject of photos, you should be alerted to the fact that this area of the business is always subject to abuse. There are many people out there who will want to list you in directories or schedule shootings with you for large amounts of money. *Don't do it!* These things will make you poorer, and will not help your career. If anyone pushes you to spend a lot of money on photos, question their motives. Some unscrupulous agencies or photographers make lots of money convincing young models who don't know any better that they need really good photos to succeed. That may sound logical, but it's not accurate. As mentioned above, the proper way to go about it is to do testing that costs little or nothing. If you can't find a photographer in your area who is willing to test you, expand your search area. Just don't spend a lot of your hard earned money on photos that you don't actually need.

If you are entering the modeling business to have fun and make some fast bucks, you should perhaps reconsider your choice of careers. For most people, becoming a successful model takes a combination of hard work, dedication and determination, on top of the physical attributes that you either have or you don't. Modeling *can* be fun and often is. Just don't expect it to be one long party. It isn't.

Once you're in the door of the agency and you've got a portfolio together, you can settle down to the real business of being a model. That's being a professional. Models get paid a lot for their services and clients will expect a lot from you in return. It becomes your business to make sure you allow plenty of time to arrive at a shooting at the proper time, and you have brought with you anything that might have been requested. You should be ready to go when they are ready for you, and have a good attitude about what you are doing. If you are good-natured and fun to be around while still being highly professional, you'll get booked again and again.

Of course, you always need to look your best. If you haven't developed good grooming habits, start now. Take care of your skin, hair and hands, and always appear at an appointment clean and neatly dressed, unless you have been told otherwise by your agent.

If you have any dispute with a client, you should leave it for your agent to handle. That's part of their job. You should be cooperative during a shooting, but if you are asked to do anything that you feel is improper, do not hesitate to call your agent.

There are many "tricks" to becoming a professional model, like learning to apply a little makeup to hide that five o'clock shadow, or how to slip out of a jacket on the runway. Never be afraid to ask questions of your agent or fellow models who have more experience. That's the best way to learn.

CHAPTER TWO

THE MODELING AGENCY

One of your first steps in becoming a model is finding a modeling agency to represent you. In the larger markets, it is impossible to work as a model without an agency. In some small cities it may be possible to work freelance, but this is becoming more and more difficult. It is much easier for clients to deal with one source of models and pay the agency directly for all the models they use.

A modeling agency usually represents many models and actively seeks work for them. They will set up go-sees with clients, and respond to casting calls or specific requests for particular models. Your agent will also negotiate your fee for each job, although in most instances, there are standard fees for different kinds of work. These fees vary widely across the United States and for that matter, the world. In all cases, the client will pay the agency, and the agency will deduct its fee (usually 15-20%) before paying you. Many agencies work on what is known as a voucher system. With this system, you get paid the following week for any work that you do. Since the agency usually doesn't get paid that fast, they charge you an extra percentage for the service. Most of the big New York agencies follow this system, and most models take advantage of it, since many clients do not pay before 90 days! It's worth the extra fee to get paid right away. In smaller cities, most agencies cannot afford to offer this service, and you will be paid after the agency receives the money.

Any legitimate agency is always interested in new faces. They are always looking for the next star model. Because of this, all agencies schedule time when they will interview new models who are interested in joining the agency. A simple phone call will let you know when that time is, and what to bring with you. When you call, you may be asked how tall you are. If you're not at least six feet tall, they may tell you not to bother coming in. Although virtually anyone who is the right height can get through the door of the agency, that's no guarantee that they'll be interested in signing you. Often there will be someone who "pre-screens" the models, only allowing the better models in to see those actually responsible for signing new models. Even if you are accepted, there's no guarantee that they'll be able to find you any work. However, a legitimate agency will not take you on unless they are pretty sure that they will be able to find work for you. After all, that's the way the agencies make money. If you aren't working, they're not making any money either.

If you are turned down by one agency, you needn't throw in the towel immediately. See some other agencies (or every agency) and get as many opinions as possible. Just because one agency doesn't feel that they can work with you doesn't mean that another one won't. If many agencies refuse you, it is possible that modeling is just not for you. Not everyone succeeds at it, and any model should be prepared to take up another form of employment in the event he can't get a modeling career off the ground.

If you are accepted by an agency, it is more than likely that they will sign you to an exclusive contract. Do not sign any contract before reading it first. If you do not understand any part of it, consult a lawyer before signing. This is very important, because there may be clauses in the contract that you may not like. If the agency says that "It's our standard contract, everybody signs it", you must still insist on reading it. That's just good common sense, but you'd be surprised to find that many people with stars in their eyes just sign on the dotted line without question, and have been quite surprised later to find they had signed a document that was more favorable to the agency than to themselves.

Although the vast majority of modeling agencies are legitimate businesses, many shady characters find that this is the ideal business to exploit to their advantage. On the surface, it may be virtually impossible to tell a good agency from a bad one, but there are ways of finding out. First, an agency that has been around for at least several years is apt to be legitimate. The unscrupulous agencies generally rip you off and leave town quickly. You can always go to the Better Business Bureau or the local Chamber of Commerce. If any complaints have been lodged against the company, you are apt to find out about it through those sources.

Legitimate agencies all work pretty much the same, at least in broad scope, and there are certain fees that they will charge the models that are commonplace. The largest fee that is likely to be charged to a model is for having one or more photographs placed in the agency book or headsheet. This fee varies widely, but usually reflects the actual cost of putting the book together. Thus, a simple headsheet should cost each model far less than an elaborate agency book would. All of the top New York agencies have elaborate books showing pictures of all of their models. These books come out at least once each year and sometimes twice. Participation by each model is required, and the fee generally varies between $500 - $1,000 per model. In other cities, the fee may be as low as $20.00, or perhaps no fee at all. A model is also responsible for having his modeling cards with his pictures on them made up, and if the agency does this, they will charge the model for it. Other fees that are likely to be charged to a model are for messengers, shipping and postage fees for shipping out portfolios or modeling cards, long distance telephone calls, telegrams, telexes, or faxes. All of the fees mentioned above are charged to the models by most agencies and are deducted from their earnings.

There are other fees that would not be considered legitimate. No agency that is really interested in representing you is going to ask for money from you up front. All the fees mentioned above are deducted from the money you will earn from modeling. If an agency doesn't think it can recover those fees in that manner, then they have no business representing you. And although an agency may set up many photography tests for you, they should all be very inexpensive. All agencies know photographers who will test for very little or no money. If the agency says that you'll need pictures that cost hundreds of dollars or more, and wants the money up front, beware! This is definitely not a good situation to be in! Yes, photographs are needed, and yes, many photographers won't work for free, but any model with potential should be able to get decent photographs through low-cost testing, not by paying a photographer big money.

After assembling your test shots and helping put your portfolio together, an agency will begin to send you out on go-sees. Generally, your agent will make many calls to clients and tell them that they have a new model that they would like to be seen by the casting department, or whoever is responsible for hiring models. These are called general go-sees and they are not for any particular job but just so the client becomes aware of you. It is very important to be on time for these appointments, as clients are generally very busy people and are doing you a favor by seeing you. When you arrive, you should be clean and neatly dressed, and you should always hand over your portfolio right side up and unzipped. The client should never have to struggle to see your pictures! You should also have your modeling cards with you so you can leave one with the client. These are usually kept on file, and many people use them for casting purposes. All they need do is go to the files and sort through the cards to find the model they like.

Many times, a go-see will be requested by a client for a job that is coming up. He may request you personally, or ask your agent to send over anyone who fits a particular physical type or age range. At these go-sees, it is not unusual for the casting director to take a Polaroid of you, or request that you wear something specific. If you are going to a go-see for a job modeling suits, it would certainly not hurt your chances to show up in one. If the job was for something casual or sporty, again dressing that way to the go-see can only help. Some casting directors (it has been said) have rather limited imaginations. If you show up looking the part of what they want, you are more likely to get the job than if they must imagine you in a different way than you present yourself.

Clients will often use your modeling card or the agency book or headsheet to find the models they need and will not bother with a preliminary go-see. They will simply call the agency and book you directly. Your agency should find out everything that will be required of you, and relay this information to you. Since bookings often come in unexpectedly, most agencies require all their models to call in at least twice each day, once in the morning, and once in the afternoon.

Whenever you have a booking, you will have the client sign a voucher with your hours on it to turn in to the agency. This voucher is used to make sure the client is billed correctly and that you are paid as well. It also has a release on it. Some clients may ask you to sign a special release, but this is usually not done without your agent being consulted first. If you are asked to sign a photo release, check with your agent to make sure that is all right to do so first.

Although getting represented by an agent can be difficult, you should remember that an agent is really a middleman who is trying to satisfy his clients. You are one of his clients.

Without the models, there is no reason for the agency to exist. Their product is you. Don't let that fact make you cocky and demanding. Just remember that they are working for you and all their other clients. Your relationship with the agency should be a good, honest one with all lines of communication open. If you feel you are not being treated well, you should talk to them about it or consider moving to another agency.

If you are so lucky as to be able to pick and choose agencies to represent you, you may have a difficult decision to make. While all agencies are basically the same in their operation, their personalities can be quite different. Some people prefer large agencies with a lot of "clout" and prestige, while others prefer small agencies that can devote a lot of time and consideration to each model. It is not unusual for models to switch agencies many times before finding the one that suits them the best.

Approaching An Agency

So you know how an agency works, now how to you get signed with one? There are many different ways that this can happen. If you are in a small town or city, the best way to find an agency is to consult your yellow pages telephone directory under the heading of "Models." Call them up and ask for an appointment. They will tell you what to bring with you (ask, if they don't tell you!). In a small market, they may require you to have a portfolio before they can do anything with you, but for your initial meeting some simple snapshots will do (like those mentioned below). In larger cities, or cities outside of your area, you should mail in some photos with a brief letter listing your statistics (height, weight, suit size, etc), and any modeling experience that you may have. Include a stamped, self-addressed envelope if you require your photos back, as most agencies receive many letters of this sort every day. The photos that you send should show you clearly. Several different shots should be included if possible, showing a close-up of your face, something active, and something to show your physique (no nudes). Do not mail in a whole portfolio if you have one. If you have one, mention in your letter with the snapshots, "portfolio available upon request." If the agency is interested, they will contact you.

When meeting with an agent for the first time, it is important that you arrive on time (most important), and that you be well-groomed and dressed neatly. Don't wear any makeup under any circumstances. If you had a tough night before your appointment, consider re-scheduling. It's better that they get the best possible impression of you. That's about all you can do. Whatever they think after that is their impression of whether or not you can be a successful model under their care. If an agency doesn't feel they can help you, don't get bent out of shape. They know their market and it's requirements. Be polite and thank them for their time. Ask them to suggest other agencies if possible, or any constructive criticism.

An agency may be immediately interested in you. If you are in a small town or city (or even a large one) and the agency also has a modeling school, they might ask you to sign up for classes (at a fee) before they will agree to represent you. If they guarantee you that you will be a working professional model after taking their classes, walk out the door and don't go back. If they are so sure that you will be a professional, you don't need the classes. If they say they will show you how to become a model through their classes and the rest is up to you, then that's a much more honest answer. They can teach anyone the things that a model must do, but no one can make a model out of someone who is not right for it. If you are 5'8" and want to be a fashion model in New York, you can take every class in the world and it will never happen. You must fit the physical requirements. No one can teach you to be six feet tall!

Agencies in big cities can have a hard time selling you unless you have a portfolio, but you should not have one made before you join an agency for the first time. The agency will help you put one together that will be best for the way they intend to "sell" you. If you already have a portfolio, your agency is likely to scrap it and start over. What a waste of money! If an agency thinks you have really great potential, they may try to set up some tests and get you working right away. In New York, or a a major city, it's much more likely that they will want you to go to Europe and get tearsheets first, before they will get you work.

CHAPTER THREE

THE PORTFOLIO

The portfolio and modeling card (also known as a composite) have been mentioned many times up to this point, but an explanation of their importance is in order. First and foremost, the portfolio and modeling card are your selling tools to get you work. There is often a considerable difference between how you look in person, and how well you photograph. Thus the portfolio is there to show the different "looks" you can achieve, and how well you work in front of the camera. Initially, all of your shots are likely to be tests, but ideally all the photographs in your book should be from actual assignments rather than tests. This shows that you are a professional working model, and the more famous the clients you have worked for are, the more favorable impression you are likely to make. A model with tearsheets from a major Calvin Klein campaign, for example, would certainly illustrate that he is a model in demand, and everyone likes to work with the top models.

The portfolio should also contain pictures showing you in different situations. There should be a headshot, a full length, a suit, something sporty and active, and always a good bathing suit or body shot to show you off. As mentioned before, your agent will help you put this all together.

Portfolios come in different sizes, and most models have one that is either 11 X 14 or possibly 8 X 10. Depending on the size and quality, expect to pay $25.00-$50.00 or more for your portfolio (without photos of course). Many New York and European models are also using what is called a "mini book" that is about 5 X 6. This smaller book is much easier to carry around (some of the bigger portfolios tend to get quite heavy!) and cheaper and easier to send through the mail. Although the book is smaller, it is just as effective as the bigger version. There are several companies that specialize in making these mini books, and will photographically reduce all of your tearsheets to fit the format. A mini book from Bookitt (see Resources for address and phone) that includes 12 photo reductions of your tears, costs about $60.00. They have mini books in sizes to accommodate up to 36 photos.

The modeling card is left behind on a go-see, or sent through the mail to prospective clients. These are usually kept on file by the person in charge of casting. These cards are about 6 X 8 and printed on heavy stock. They may be in black & white or color, and printed on one or two sides. Many models have cards that fold out into several pages with many pictures on them and are film laminated, making for a very elaborate (and quite expensive) card. A simple black & white card may cost you as little as $150.00, but an elaborate one that folds out and is in color could easily cost $6,000.00 or more. Customarily, some of a model's best pictures from his portfolio are reproduced on his card, and like the portfolio, should include a variety of shots. This card may be used for up to two years before it is considered out of date, but most models update them once or twice each year. Beginning models may have two or more different cards the first year, as the first one is apt to be thrown together in a hurry just to have something to leave with the client. A photocopy is often used in place of a card at the very beginning, but these are mostly of poor quality, and their use should be discontinued as soon as a preliminary card is ready.

The composite is becoming more and more important these days, as many casting directors simply do not have the time to leaf through an entire portfolio. They neeed to see whatever it is they are looking for very quickly and the composite fullfills this need very well. Many casting sessions are done directly from a client's file of modeling cards. This is why it is a good idea to "make the rounds" often, especially whenever you have a new card, so they can keep their files updated, and remember you.

Because a model may be in demand, and many people will want to see his portfolio at the same time, it is not unusual for each model to have several portfolios. These may not all be quite the same, and will usually be numbered in order of importance. Your #1 book would have all your best tears in it, #2 might be missing some of the better ones, but have others, etc. Sometimes models also have different books geared to specific requirements. One book may be geared more heavily toward fashion, while another may be more sporty. The appropriate one would be sent to the proper client. Most portfolios, however, show as wide a range as possible, since it is usually impossible to second guess what a client may be looking for. Some models find it smart to have more than one composite. Stan Newman, who is interviewed in the second section of this book, currently has two different ones. On the advice of his agent, he made a special card that features his hands for the purpose of getting work as a hand model. He has found that it has easily paid for itself with the additional work he has gotten in that category.

Because the portfolio is such a powerful selling tool, the pictures contained in it take on major importance. Every model eventually wants to get booked for advertising or catalog jobs, because those are the ones that pay the most. Generally, clients like to see models with really great books, and testing alone usually doesn't supply this. The best way to get great photos by top photographers is to work with magazines (editorial work). Magazines pay poorly, but the tearsheets obtained from the magazines can be worth more than their weight in gold to a model. Unfortunately, there is not a great deal of editorial work available to the male model in the United States. This is the main reason that many beginning models (or models seeking up-to-date tears) head for Europe.

Magazines are much more plentiful in Europe, and it is therefore much easier to obtain editorial work there than in the United States. It is not unusual for a modeling agency in New York to tell a new model that they are interested in him, but he should go to Europe and "get some good tears" first. If the agent is very interested in you, he might help to put you in contact with some European agents and get your career going. In most cases, however, you are on your own unless you are actually signed by your agent, and he has a good working relationship with a European agency. Europe will be discussed in another chapter.

As you receive more and more tears from your jobs, you will be constantly updating your portfolio and modeling card. Although you will probably have favorite photos that will remain in your portfolio for many years, the bulk of the photos should be recent. This shows that you are constantly working and in demand. Being in demand not only gets you more work, but it puts your agent in a good negotiating position to obtain better fees for you.

CHAPTER FOUR

DIET & EXERCISE

As a professional model, it is your responsibility to keep in tip-top shape. Late night parties, drugs, and poor grooming will not be tolerated by your agent or clients. When you report for work, you always must look your very best. With booking rates fast approaching $500.00 *per hour* in the top markets (plus usage fees), it should come as no surprise that a client will expect only the very best from you. A model with dark circles under his eyes from lack of sleep, or constant lateness will not exactly endear him to his employers. They have a right to expect you to show up on time and looking *great!*

Looking great requires a concentrated effort. Eating well, exercising, plenty of sleep, and good grooming are pretty much a full-time job in their own right. A guy in his early twenties may feel that all of that stuff comes naturally, and indeed, much of it can. However, as a man grows older, he will find that more and more time will be needed to be spent on keeping up his good looks, especially if he has left it to chance in the past. The best time to start a good health & fitness regimen is *now*. Don't wait until you start to slow down or begin noticing extra wrinkles to start taking care of yourself. It only gets more difficult.

Eating Right

Good health starts with what you put in your body. Our bodies require six nutrients, and those are carbohydrates, fats, protein, vitamins, minerals, and water. These contain chemical substances that function in one or more of the following three ways: they furnish the body with energy, they provide material for growth and repair of body tissues, and they assist in the regulation of body processes. Although every nutrient has its own specific functions, no nutrient acts totally independently of other nutrients. All the nutrients must be present in the diet in varying quantities and proportions in order to sustain life.

Of the six nutrients, carbohydrates, fats, and proteins are the primary sources of energy. Their energy value is expressed as calories.

Carbohydrates are the largest supplier of energy for all body functions and muscular exertion. They are necessary for proper digestion, especially in breaking down fat. Approximately 55%-60% of our calorie intake should consist of carbohydrates.

Fats are the most *concentrated* source of energy in our diet, furnishing over twice as many calories per gram (9) than proteins or carbohydrates (4). The sole *essential* use of fat is as a source of fatty acids which are necessary to all cells and tissues of the body. Fats also aid in the proper utilization of vitamins, among other functions. Fats should make up approximately 25%-30% of our calories.

Protein is of primary importance in the development and growth of all body tissues. It is the major source of building material for muscles, blood, skin, hair, nails, and all the internal organs. The average American gets far more protein in his diet than is necessary. Only about 10%-15% of our calories should be made up of protein.

Vitamins, while essential to our health, remain more of a mystery than the other nutrients. Vitamins work with enzymes in the body, which have numerous essential functions. So far, 13 vitamins have been identified as being essential to proper nutrition, although many experts argue about the quantity of vitamin intake necessary for good health. The 13 vitamins are: A, the B complex vitamins (Thiamin, Riboflavin, Pantothenic acid, Niacin, B-6, Biotin, Folacin, and B-12), C, D, E and K.

Minerals, like vitamins, act as catalysts for many biological functions in the body. Minerals are important components of the bones and teeth, as well as the soft tissues, muscles, and blood. Many different minerals, in varying proportions, are required by the body, but only a few are likely to be undersupplied. These are calcium, iron and iodine.

About two-thirds of the body weight consists of water, and is our most important nutrient. It is either directly responsible for, or involved in nearly every bodily function.

The United States Government has set standards for what they believe to be the recommended daily requirement for nutrients, also known as *USRDA*. These are officially defined as "the levels of intake of essential nutrients considered, in the judgment of the Food and Nutrition Board on the basis of available scientific knowledge, to be adequate to meet the known nutritional needs of practically all healthy persons." Many scientists dispute these standards as too low, but you can use them as a jumping off point.

We have heard that a "proper diet" contains all sorts of nutrients, and it's important that we get all these things in the proper quantities. Short of going to college, how will be ever learn just what is a proper diet? Actually, it's not as difficult as that. This is where all those "food groups" come in that you've heard about. "Food groups" are merely categories of food that are similar, and there are four main ones. These are: milk and milk by-products (such as cheese, butter, yogurt, etc.), meats (including red meats, fish, poultry, and eggs), fruits and vegetables, and lastly, cereals or grains. Nutrients are present in all these food groups, but in varying types and quantities. Since there is no single "perfect food" (one that contains all the nutrients essential to life), you must eat many foods to insure that you receive all the nutrients that you need. By making your diet varied, you will insure that you receive all the nutrients that you ever need. This need for a varied diet is exactly why the fad diets consisting heavily of one food like pineapples or grapefruits can be dangerous. Avoid fad diets at all costs.

A proper diet should also exclude or limit things that are either unnecessary or harmful in certain quantities. Cholesterol is one of those items right at the top of most doctor's lists. However, cholesterol is essential to the body, and in fact, our bodies *manufacture it*. Scientific research has shown that too high a concentration of cholesterol in the blood can cause serious problems, including a high possibility of heart attack. The level of cholesterol in the blood is normally kept constant by a balance of the sum of it taken in the diet plus that manufactured by the body, and the amount used up in the body or excreted. Thus, diet alone may not be able to control the amount of cholesterol in the bloodstream. To play safe however, we should limit the amount of cholesterol in our diet, as there is little danger that we will not get enough.

Dietary supplements are all the rage now, but unless your doctor specifically prescribes them for you, you are more than likely wasting considerable amounts of money. The source of vitamins, fiber, protein, minerals, and any number of other things that are offered to us in strange little pills, *should be from the food that we eat*. After all, that is the *main function* of eating to begin with. If you are concerned that you are not getting all the nutrients that you require, instead of taking a pill, eat some good wholesome food. The fresher the better. It's cheaper, and more pleasurable as well, than processed foods. There is absolutely no proof that large doses of vitamins will cure anything. There *is* proof that overdoses of some vitamins and minerals can be toxic to the body. Other vitamins (like vitamin C) are not stored in the body and excess amounts of it are simply eliminated. Overdoses of those vitamins are just plain wasteful.

There are times when dietary supplements may become necessary for some people, who cannot get all the nutrients that they require no matter what foods they eat. If you feel that you have this problem, see your doctor for advice.

Exercise

Today's culture is very body conscious. This means that models need to be in great physical shape. For most models, this generally means regular workouts at a gym, or lots of sports activities. Most active guys do both, but it is often easier for a busy model to spare an hour to get to the gym, than to schedule sports activities that may require travel or elaborate equipment.

If you have a weight problem, this must be given your immediate attention. A model who doesn't fit into the clothes isn't likely to get booked for the job. Although there can be quite a bit of latitute in sizing, the generally accepted suit size for a male model is 40 regular (the most frequent sample size),and a 30-32 inch waist is the most common. Naturally, all models don't fit squarely into these sizes, but the closer you are, the more work you're likely to get.

If you do need to drop some weight, your diet and exercise plan should be a careful one. Crash diets are unhealthy and can leave you with no energy. A model needs all the energy he can get!

Just about any exercise that will increase your heartbeat is a start in the right direction. Elevating the heartbeat to 65% to 85% of its capacity for a sustained period of not fewer than 20 minutes is a way of improving the cardiovascular/respiratory system, which in turn will increase your body's ability to utilize oxygen, and to burn calories. It will also ease the burden on your heart, as the increased capacity allows the heart to pump more blood with each stroke. Regular exercise also helps lower blood pressure, and researchers have shown that active people have less cholesterol accumulations in the arteries.

Exercises that specifically work on improving the cardio-vascular system are called *Aerobic*. Finding your target heart rate for aerobic exercise can be done by taking your maximum heart rate of 220, subtracting your age, and then multiplying by .65 for your lower limit, or .85 for your upper limit. To check your heart rate, pause briefly from your exercise and take your pulse immediately by feeling the artery in your wrist. Count the number of beats in ten seconds and multiply by six. This will give you the number of heartbeats per minute. After about 15 seconds of rest your heartbeat will slow down and will not give you an accurate measurement, so make sure that you do it immediately. Beginners should start at the lower end of the scale (65%) and gradually work their way up (to a maximum of 85%).

Aerobic exercise has become very popular, and we've heard these exercises referred to as *Aerobics*, *Low-Impact Aerobics*, or even *No-Impact Aerobics*. Exactly what is the difference? The key word is impact, and it refers directly to the amount of stress put upon your body during exercise. More specifically, it is the stress on your joints, such as the knees and ankles, and the skeletal system in general, as well as the muscles. Regular aerobics, or Aerobic Dancing, with much jumping around, is considered to be the most stressful, and many exercise gurus such as Jane Fonda are now advocating the less stressful low-impact aerobics. Low-impact aerobics generally involve a workout that leaves one foot on the floor at all times, easing the stress on the body. No-impact aerobics usually involve no jumping around of any kind. Jake Steinfeld's exercise program, *Body By Jake*, advocates the no-impact workout. Yoga is another example of a no-impact workout, as is bicycling. Don't think, however, that low-impact or no-impact aerobics are less strenuous or easier than regular aerobics. They may take a slower pace, but are still excellent workouts.

All of these workouts are tough for the beginner, and should be eased into slowly. Even for the well-trained, one should always ease into and out of their exercise program with a warm-up and a cool-down period, which often is a lighter version of the exercise that you plan to do. This helps avoid stress on the system, and generally improves the benefits of the workout. Stretching should only be a *part* of the warm-up or cool-down. Do not stretch your muscles when they are cold, as they are very inelastic in this state. Only when the blood-flow increases and warms the muscles do they become more flexible. Avoid any bouncing or over-stretching as this can cause the muscles to contract and shorten, which is the opposite of what you wish to accomplish. Stretching properly increases the mobility of the muscles, making them more flexible and less injury prone.

As we improve our cardiovascular system, we increase our metabolism. Metabolism is the conversion of nutrients into energy and building material for the tissues. This liberation of energy from nutrients is expressed as calories. Increasing the metabolism increases the rate in which calories are "burned off." Studies have shown that regular exercise increases overall body metabolism for up to 24 hours after the actual workout. Thus, exercising regularly will help burn off calories at a higher rate, and at an increased rate throughout the day, even while we are at rest.

The type of exercise or exercises that you choose for yourself can depend on many factors. Some people are limited by time, space, equipment, transportation, location, and other factors. You are more likely to stick with an exercise program

PHOTO BY ERIC PERKINS

Stretching should be part of your warm-up.

that you enjoy. The best plan is the one that suits your individual needs. Combining exercise with other activities is a good way to get around a time limitation. Bicycling is good exercise as well as transportation. Many models ride their bicycles all over New York City going from one appointment to the next. It's faster than most other forms of transportation in the city and quite a bit cheaper too. Jogging is another efficient way to get from one place to the next, but limit this activity to times before or after your appointments. It won't do to show up at a booking all sweaty!

Riding a stationary bicycle while watching TV or catching up on reading is another efficient way of combining activities. Many exercise bikes fold right up and you can store them in a small amount of space. If you cannot afford any equipment, you might want to exercise along with a program on TV, an audio cassette or record, or one of many books. If a place to swim or jog is handy, no equipment is necessary. If you hate to exercise alone, yet can't afford to join a health club or take classes, perhaps you can convince a friend or a family member to exercise with you. Working together can be a lot of fun, and you may find yourself exercising for a longer period of time.

The important fact to remember is to exercise regularly. For a beginner, three times per week should suffice, but six times should be the maximum as you grow stronger. Start out slowly and ease your way into your program. Don't overextend yourself by trying to do too much too soon. Your body will be much healthier if you condition it properly. Perhaps you would like to cross-train by trying many different kinds of exercise for variety's sake. Maybe you'll settle on cross-country skiing in the Winter, jogging in the Spring and Fall, and swimming in the Summer. You can get great workouts from any or all of these.

After you have settled into your regular program of exercise, you'll probably notice increased vigor, an improved mental outlook, and a general sense of well-being. This can be great for a model who must constantly put up with intense competition and rejection. Muscle tone should also be greatly improved. One note of interest is that there is no such thing as spot-toning. If you have excess fat in one specific area (like the mid-section) that you wish to reduce, all the sit-ups in the world won't make a difference. Exercise tones the muscles, not the fat. Any exercise, done properly, will help you lose weight all over, by speeding up the metabolism, which does burn fat. When you exercise, expect to lose fat from all areas of the body.

Lets look at some of the benefits and drawbacks of varying types of exercise:

WALKING

Walking is great exercise for virtually everyone, and offers proof positive that exercise does not need to be strenuous to yield results. You will burn just as many calories walking a mile as you would jogging the same mile, although you will not receive the same aerobic benefits, and it will take you longer to walk than to run. Walking requires no equipment other than good footwear, and is unlikely to cause any injuries. Walking promotes weight loss, helps relieve stress, improves mood and mental functions, and may drastically decrease your chance of heart disease.

If you do decide to start with walking, use a brisk stride. Keep your head, neck and back erect, and keep your stomach and buttocks pulled in. Look straight ahead, and swing your arms for more power and balance. Don't forget to breath regularly. Wear loose comfortable clothing that will allow perspiration to evaporate.

JOGGING

Jogging or running is more efficient exercise than walking, requires less time to achieve the same benefits, and is an excellent aerobic workout. However, stress related injuries are more frequent. Common injuries involve the bones, ligaments, muscles, tendons, and cartilage. Avoid many of these injuries by warming up properly and stretching. Warm-ups and cool-downs will relieve a lot of the stress involved in jogging. Proper footwear is an absolute must. Jogging shoes should be flexible, with well-cushioned soles, and wide built-up heels. Running on softer surfaces like dirt, as opposed to concrete, may ease some of the stress as well.

AEROBICS

Aerobics is a name given to a regimen of exercises that condition the body in an aerobic manner. These exercises are usually done with little or no equipment, and are often choreographed to music. Calisthenics, jazz, ballet and disco-style dancing may all be integrated into the workout. Aerobics, as we have seen, come in three different forms: Regular, Low-Impact, and No-Impact. Regular aerobics involve much jumping around. Aerobic dancing fits in this category. For burning calories, Regular Aerobics may be great, but it is also the most stressful of the three. Low-Impact Aerobics are less stressful on the body, yet still have high benefits. Jane Fonda and many others have programs available in book and video form that stress Low-Impact workouts. No-Impact Aerobics afford the lowest stress to the body. One proponent of No-Impact Aerobics is Jake Steinfeld, and his workout is available on video cassette.

PHOTO BY ERIC PERKINS

Jogging is great exercise.

YOGA

Yoga is not known as an aerobic workout, yet done properly, it is. It also is of the no-impact variety. An added benefit of Yoga is that one meditates while doing it, so it may ease stress and relax you. Many people think that because of its Far Eastern origins, yoga is religious in nature. It isn't, unless that is what one wishes to gain from it. Yoga philosophy holds that mind and body are interdependent. Hatha Yoga is the form that gives its attention to the physical body. All movements are done slowly and are based on the formula of stretching, relaxation, deep breathing, increasing circulation, and concentration. Although there are as many as 840,000 yoga poses, most people practice a relative few of them. Position of the body is important, so it is a good idea to learn the techniques from someone well-practiced in the art. Avoid overstretching as it can damage your muscles. Yoga is something that takes a while to learn properly, so don't rush into it. One major benefit of Yoga is that it can be done virtually anywhere, with no equipment.

CYCLING

Bicycle riding is another form of a no-impact workout. It can be done outside, or inside with a stationary cycling machine. The choice is up to you on which you prefer: they both offer the same aerobic benefits. Done properly, cycling has all the aerobic benefits of running, and virtually none of the stress-related injuries. The equipment necessary is more expensive than many of the other forms of exercise, and if you live in a small apartment, you may not have the room for it either. While cycling, remember to follow the rules of the road, and keep your bike in tip top condition to avoid accidents.

The first step toward proper cycling is having the correct equipment. It is essential that your bike "fits" you properly. As

The Lifecycle is a good alternative to a bicycle.

every body comes in different sizes, so do bicycles. Most bikes are adjustable and it is important that you take the time to size them correctly.

ROWING

Rowing can be done on land or water, and is an excellent aerobic workout. This is a low stress workout that works many of the muscle groups. As in cycling, the equipment can take up a lot of space and is not inexpensive.

Although the arms drive the oars, the thighs provide much of the power. The seat slides back and forth, so that as you pull the oars toward yourself, the legs straighten out, pushing the seat backwards. As you push the oars back away you draw your knees up, bringing the seat forward and back to the starting position. If you are using a rowing shell on the water, as opposed to a rowing machine, you need to develop your balance and remain relaxed. A smooth rhythm yields the best results on land or water.

SWIMMING

Swimming can be an excellent workout for all the major muscle groups of the body, and has a very low injury rate. Whereas running and cycling primarily develop the lower body, swimming mostly develops the upper body. Because water relieves much of gravity related stress, swimming is an ideal workout for those people who are overweight or suffering from lower back or knee problems. The aerobic benefits are almost on a par with both running and cross-country skiing (excellent). Your target heart rate will be slightly lower for swimming.

Subtract your age from 205 instead of the usual 220 and multiply by .65 to .85 as before.

For the best training effect, you should swim at least 25 yards without turning. Turning usually gives you a little rest, which subtracts from the value of the workout. If you are using your back-yard pool, it is probably not that long, and you will find yourself turning frequently. Try not to slow down on these occasions, and keep up your pace.

PHOTO COURTESY OF BALLY FITNESS PRODUCTS

Excellent rowing machines are now available.

As in all exercise, technique plays an essential role in swimming. Stroke, breathing and kicking are all important elements. If you do not know how to swim properly, it is recommended that you learn from a professional instructor, so that you may receive full benefit from your efforts.

CROSS-COUNTRY SKIING

Cross-country, or Nordic, skiing develops more muscles of the body than any other sport, and as such, makes it the best aerobic activity available. This will burn off the calories at a terrific rate, without causing much stress. Beginners can bene-fit from cross-country skiing, but must take the time to learn the proper techniques involved. Equipment is generally less expensive than downhill skiing, and the injury rate is far lower. Proper clothing is very important.

Nordic skiing requires the practitioner to use muscles in the arms, legs and trunk in nearly equal measure. This gives the body a good overall musculature. Proper technique involves balance, weight shift, and kicking. The arms also play an important role. Cross-country skiing is done mainly on flat land or gentle inclines. The motions involved most resemble a combination of running and ice skating.

WEIGHT TRAINING

Weight training will build and delineate the muscles, and is strictly for looks (and strength). Having a well developed body does not guarantee good health. Health and appearance can be two widely different things. Weight training is rarely aerobic unless done continuously, with no more than 15 seconds of rest between sets. If you've ever been in a crowded gym, you'll know that this can be virtually impossible.

PHOTO COURTESY OF NORDIC TRACK

Cross-country skiing is the best aerobic exercise.

PHOTO COURTESY OF ADIDAS

Weight training defines and tones the muscles.

A man wishing to become a model may well want to do some weight training, as the results are flattering to the male body, and important for many modeling assignments. However, it is important that one does not over-train. Remember, a male model should be able to fit into a size 40 regular suit, and that can be tough to do with over-developed muscles.

Weight training can be accomplished on either machines or by using free-weights. There is less danger of injury when using machines, but proper instruction is essential for either method.

On The Go

Going on location can wreck absolute havoc with any diet and exercise program, but you don't have to let it. As you become a seasoned model and a world traveler, you'll get to know a lot about the exercise possibilities away from home. Many hotels around the world now have in-hotel fitness centers, or make arrangements for their guests with nearby gyms. Additionally, many resort hotels, where models are likely to find themselves, have extensive grounds and jogging trails that run through them.

Jogging can be done anywhere, from the beaches of the Caribbean, to the mountains of Peru. But be cautious! Breathing can be difficult in high altitudes, so you'll want to take it especially easy.

If you're trapped in a gloomy big city hotel on a rainy day, you can try walking up the stairs, rather than use the elevator. That can be some workout! You could bring an audio tape of your favorite aerobic workout, and go it alone in your room, or bring along lightweight workout equipment specially designed with traveling in mind.

Whatever exercise you plan to undertake while on the road, try to schedule it into your routine so that you won't get lazy and put it off until the last minute. When you're working hard away from home, you may find exercise is just the pickup you need to maintain your energy and feel good about yourself.

Take the exercise or exercises of your choice and build your own personal routine, remembering to start easy and work your way up. Coupled with your own reducing diet (if need be), you'll start to look and feel more like the model you wish to be.

CHAPTER FIVE

LOOKING GREAT

When you're young, good grooming may mean washing your face and combing your hair. A model usually doesn't get off so easily. He must always be ready to face the camera. When the camera moves in for a close-up, any flaws that are visible are going to be magnified.

Some models may take a do-it-yourself attitude when it comes to good grooming, but for some, professional help is clearly in order. If the skin or hair is in poor condition, experimenting on it yourself is probably not the best idea. Most models, however, should be able to take care of the day-to-day upkeep of their skin and hair with only occasional visits to the pros.

When it comes to skin care products, it is best to select ones based on your skin type. There is such a variety of products available, that it will probably be necessary to test several of them to find the one that works best for you. A short cut to this process is to ask other models or makeup artists what they use. But because various products may react to each skin type differently, there's no guarantee that a product will work equally well for you as it does for someone else.

Just about everyone will tell you to use products that are low in alcohol content. Alcohol robs the skin of its moisture, leaving it tight, dry, and lifeless. Deodorant soap can have the same effect if used on the face, as it can be too harsh. When cleaning the face, use a soap or liquid cleanser that's designed for that purpose.

Everyone loves a good "healthy" tan, but as you may already know, overexposure to the sun is far from healthy. Prolonged exposure to the sun can cause irreparable damage to your skin by dehydrating it and causing wrinkles to form, thus speeding up the aging process. This doesn't mean that you should necessarily stay out of the sun, but rather prepare your skin for it. Always wear a sunscreen, making sure you reapply it after swimming or sweating. The SPF (sun protection factor) of the sunscreen is expressed in numbers; the higher the number, the more protection.

Because frequent exposure to the sun also causes water loss through perspiration, remember to replace it by drinking several glasses of water each day. When you're on location, remember that the strength of the sun varies in different parts of the world. Generally, the further south you travel, or the closer to the equator, the stronger the sun will be. Just because you arrive in Barbados with a deep tan doesn't mean that you can't still get a burn under its tropical sun. You can! Overcast days also don't necessarily offer much protection. The burning rays of the sun can penetrate the cloud cover very easily.

Remember, too, that the effects of the sun may not be visible right away, but will start to become more and more evident as you grow older. Unfortunately, by the time you begin to notice the effects, the damage has been done and can't be reversed.

Cold weather can also dry out the skin, and ultraviolet reflection from snow can cause sunburn every bit as painful and damaging as you experienced on the beach. Moisturizing and taking care of your skin is a year 'round affair.

Although shaving is a major source of irritation for many men, remember that there are very few models with facial hair. That makes regular shaving mandatory, although not necessarily every day. Many skin problems are the result of shaving. An unsanitary or dull razor, inadequate lubrication and even aftershave lotions may aggravate the skin. On days that you are not working, you might want to skip shaving to give your face a break. If your beard is not too heavy, you may find that an electric razor will be more gentle to your face than a safety razor. Remember, the closest shave is *not* necessarily the best! Many models have made a career out of the scruffy "five o'clock shadow" look, but most will come clean instantly if necessary for a booking. Other models with very heavy beards never seem to be able to get a close enough shave, and often have to resort to makeup as a coverup for some jobs.

Hair is one of the most important features of a male model, and more than one career has receded as quickly as the hairline. Top models generally have great looking heads of hair. Just as there are different skin types, there are also different hair types. Dry hair may require frequent conditioning, and oily hair frequent washing. If you are using hair gels, foams or sprays for styling purposes, you will probably need to wash your hair more frequently than if you don't. These products can clog pores on the scalp and actually *attract* dirt, resulting ultimately in damage to the hair.

Besides keeping your hair cleaned and conditioned, you'll need to have a good professional cut. Basically, a model will probably want to keep his hair on the long side, so that it is versatile and can be styled in different ways to achieve many "looks". Some models have very long hair or very short hair, and while both looks are very "in" today, having those hairstyles will limit the amount of work you do. Fortunately, hair is easily cut and restyled or grown longer to suit the changing fashions.

Another important feature of a model is his hands. If you don't know how to give yourself a good manicure, it's time you learned. A model's hands are frequently in the picture, and the better they look, the more often you'll be booked for those shots. Some models have such great looking hands that they make it a specialty, having *only* their hands appear in the picture. For more on this and other specialties, see Chapter Seven.

CHAPTER SIX

WORKING ABROAD

These days, virtually all new models, male or female, will begin their professional careers with a trip abroad. The most likely destinations are Japan, Italy, France, Germany, Australia, and England. Most male models start out in Paris or Milan. The reason for this travel is simple: to build the portfolio and gain experience.

Working abroad offers many opportunities that working at home cannot. Although New York is probably the world's center of fashion modeling, there is less editorial work there than in other parts of the world, especially for men. Editorial (magazine) work is generally the most creative and yields the best portfolio pictures, although it pays very little. Europe has far more magazines, and thus much more editorial work for male models, than does the United States. The U.S. does have much more high paying advertising work to offer, so most models head to Europe to build their portfolios in order to return to the U.S. and snag the high paying advertising jobs. Some models do elect to stay in Europe for extended periods of time because they find it easier to work there than in the United States. A model can make a very good living there, especially if he is right for catalog work, of which there is quite a bit.

Many models just starting out will come to New York and be told the same thing by all the agencies they see. "You have a good look, but you need better pictures in your portfolio. Come back and see us after you've been to Europe." Sometimes, if the agency thinks a model is really great, they will take him on and help arrange the trip to Europe (although it's still unlikely that they will pay for it) and upon his return will decide on the basis of his tears whether to take him on permanently. Without an American agency backing you, getting to Europe can be a tough, eye-opening experience, but many men have done it successfully.

If an agent suggests that you take a trip to Europe, get as much information as you can. What city do they recommend? (Probably Paris or Milan). Will they contact an agency in that city for you and help set it up? Will they at least recommend some legitimate agencies for you to contact once you're there? The amount of information they give you will generally be in direct proportion to how interested they are in you. The more information they give you, the more interested you can assume them to be. If they say, "oh, just contact any of the agencies over there" you can assume they are not that interested in you, at least at present. That doesn't necessarily mean they won't be interested when you get back.

When heading for a foreign country, it's best to find out everything you can about that country before you go. If you're going to Paris or Milan, remember that everyone is not going to speak English, and if you can learn a little French or Italian before you arrive, it would be a definite asset. A good tour guide and map are also essential. Naturally, the money is different, and getting around in an unfamiliar city can be a nightmare at first. Your trip may easily last a month or more, so remember to purchase a round trip ticket (you wouldn't want to be stranded in a foreign land) and bring sufficient money with you. "Sufficient money" is at least $1,500 - $2,000 at the time of this writing.

Be warned that most countries do not welcome foreign workers and many permits will be necessary for you to work there legally (the same is true of the United States for foreigners). In fact, if you arrive and declare you are there for modeling, they may just deport you right then and there! It is best to enter the country as a tourist. But it's not that easy to fool Immigration. If they spy your portfolio, they are smart enough to know exactly what it's for, and out you go. One model entering a foreign country was entering as a tourist, without a portfolio or *any* pictures but had a telex asking him to come for work. You guessed it! The customs official read the telex while looking through his luggage and the model was not allowed to enter the country because he did not have working papers!

After you're in the foreign country, you will find that most agencies are not interested in obtaining working papers for you. It is a lot of work and an incredible hassle. They are more than willing to help you work illegally however, and that is exactly what most models do. In return for this, the modeling agency will generally take a 50% fee on all your bookings (the standard agency fee in the U.S. is 20%). This is S.O.P. (Standard Operating Procedure) so don't be surprised by it. If you do go through the proper procedures for your working papers, you will probably find the working conditions better if you plan to stay for an extended period. As far as this goes, you should probably follow the advice of your agency.

Your main objective once you land on foreign soil is to find an agency to represent you. Generally, they will be able to help you find accommodations (usually sharing an apartment with other models) that will be more affordable than a hotel. This should be done as soon as possible as your funds are probably limited and will need to be stretched out as long as possible. With the magazines paying very low rates, and the agency taking up to 50%, don't expect to earn much money. The most important thing to do is to get work and tearsheets for your portfolio.

Assuming that you are able to find an agency that is willing to take you on, your next step will be to have a modeling card made up and to start go-sees. You have to be very on top of things, because agents in Europe are not quite as "driven" as they are here in the States. You will probably find it necessary to push for go-sees if you cannot afford to stay in Europe for an extended period of time. Their attitude is much more casual, although just as serious. Many models prefer this slower pace and end up staying for years, traveling all over. This can be especially great if you are young and have never been exposed to any culture outside of home.

CHAPTER SEVEN

OTHER TYPES OF MODELING

The word *model* usually conjures up an image of someone who is tall, well-built and incredibly handsome. That's the popular image of modeling and *is* a large segment of the business. However, there is much more to the modeling industry than just that.

These tall handsome men do most of the fashion modeling that there is, but usually do every other category as well. This versatility is what makes a model the most successful. The more categories you can fit into, the more work you'll get. Many models, however, do not do fashion modeling, but make a very good, or even excellent, living doing other types of work.

Whereas there is a limited market for large-size and petite female models, there is no market for men in this category at all. Regular sized models fulfill all of the requirements of fashion modeling for men. Even ads for clothing for tall men are filled by regular models.

But if you are young or old, short or tall, fat or thin, handsome or just ordinary, you still might be a model. Just as real people come in all shapes and sizes, so do models. You've seen them yourself. Open up any magazine and turn to a non-fashion advertisement. All the people you see in the ads are professional models. This is called commercial print modeling and is open to all types. Here it is more important that you have the right look for the job, not how tall or handsome you are (except when that's the type they're looking for!) Just like in any other field of modeling, the competition can be intense. In fact, since just about anyone might be in competition with you, it can actually be *more* difficult to survive on this kind of modeling. Console yourself with the fact that there are more jobs of this type than any other, and if you really work hard at it, you will get repeat business from clients who appreciate you. If you have a very "all-American" look, that is essentially blond hair with blue eyes, your chances of working successfully in commercial print are excellent. If you are very off-beat, you may find success as well, but it will be more limited unless you get lucky. The actor who is versatile enough to portray the handsome football star, the guy next door, and the geek from the science lab, will always be able to find work.

Many models who work in commercial print are freelance and do not work through only one agent, although on some occasions (especially if they are very successful) a model will be asked to sign exclusively with one agency. Mostly, however, they are registered with many agencies, and the agent getting them the work will get the commission. Some times the different agents may be in the same city and be in competition with each other, but many times they are spread out in different, perhaps nearby, cities.

Commercial print modeling doesn't always require a portfolio (although it is always a good idea), but a good headshot is mandatory. This could be 8 X 10 or 5 X 7 and you will want to have a quantity of them made up that you can send out and leave behind on interviews. These are often accompanied by resumes that list your statistics, your union affiliations, recent clients, and of course, your name and phone number (many models use answering services and print that number on their cards instead of their home number). Some commercial models have composites made, although not all of them do, especially if they are primarily actors, but it seems that the most successful models all have them.

The people who do best in this category are actors, or have acting ability, because animation and expressiveness are required. The emphasis in commercial print modeling is on the product. This is good, because the model wants to remain as anonymous as possible. If you are strongly identified with one product, other advertisers may not hire you. If you are actually a spokesman for a single product, an advertiser will usually pay you extra to be exclusive with them, at least for a particular type of product like a car or a beverage, etc.

Commercial print models also work in television commercials, which pay very well. Here your acting ability is a must, since you are not just posing for a still picture. To do TV commercials on a regular basis, you will have to join a union, usually AFTRA or SAG (or both). SAG is also the union for movie actors.

Although there is work just about anywhere for commercial print models, a move to a major city such as New York, Chicago or Los Angeles would probably be necessary to support yourself on a full-time basis. The best models in this category will register with many agencies in many different cities and do a lot of traveling. The model who is willing to go where the work is has the best chances of success.

Most runway and showroom modeling is handled by fashion models, but there is more leeway here. To do these kinds of modeling wearing the proper size is of the utmost importance. Thus a man who has the proper attitude and is the perfect size may have a good opportunity here even if he is not as handsome as other models, or doesn't photograph as well. The important thing here is to sell the clothes, and a look that may not photograph well may be perfect on the runway. On the runway, men can get away with much more than can women. While a women must appear supremely coordinated, a little awkwardness in a man can work. However, whatever a man does on the runway should be appropriate to what he is wearing. Obviously, the "awkward look" that might work well for casual clothes, will appear out of place while modeling formal attire. Another important part of modeling on the runway is attitude. Always, you should act like you own the clothes that you are wearing. You should appear comfortable in them, and give the impression that you feel you look good in them, even if you would never wear them in real life. Relating to the audience is also important, and again, you take you cue from the clothing (or the director of the show). Your direction may be "be cool and aloof", but you will want to convey that feeling in a manner that will not alienate the audience, but make them like you.

Showroom modeling requires you to basically be the correct size, but there is more to it than that. Like runway modeling, you must appear at home in the clothing. You must be well prepared with shoes and accessories, because these are rarely supplied. You should also be a man of few words, as talking to the client is not your job. Leave that to the salesman. You may wear many different outfits, many different times in the course of a day doing showroom work. Therefore, you should be well organized, so you can change into any outfit at a moment's notice.

Another type of modeling involves close-ups of different body parts. The most well known type of this modeling is hand modeling. Naturally, great looking hands are a must, with a perfect manicure. A few models (very few) specialize in this kind of work and are in great demand if they are skilled enough. Skill *is* a factor as many hand modeling jobs require a certain amount of dexterity and tiring repetition. You may have to hold your hands in a completely unnatural way to make them appear the most natural, for very long periods of time without moving.

Hand modeling is not the only type of parts modeling. Just about any body part (an eye, and ear, a foot, an elbow, etc) may be required for a shooting, and the client will probably be just as demanding as he would be for a beauty shot. Most models who have excellent body parts say so on their resumes or composites. Along with their skills they might add the phrase "excellent hands and feet," or whatever to let clients know about this specialty. This field of endeavor can encompass all models whether they are fashion or commercial types.

Knowing the type of modeling you are best suited for can save you a lot of heartbreak. There are many men who are determined to be fashion models even though they don't fit the height requirements. They are bound to be disappointed. If you read this book, you'll know where you best fit in and will go after that segment of the market. And remember, not everyone is suited to the modeling profession. It's not all glamor. In fact, most of the glamor is just an illusion. What the profession really consists of is hard work and lots of determination, no matter what category of modeling you pursue.

CHAPTER EIGHT

THE MODELING SCHOOL

There is a great amount of debate about the usefulness of modeling schools, and there is no easier way to start an argument among modeling professionals then to begin a conversation with "What do you think about modeling schools?"

A modeling school is neither good nor bad in and of itself. As in anything else, there are good ones and bad ones. The issue is further clouded by the fact that a person can become a highly successful model without ever attending one. Many people, believe it or not, take easily to modeling and, if they are right physically, can pick up everything else on the job. The catching point, and there always is one, is that everyone is not that versatile, and many people do not have the faintest idea of what modeling is really about or the discipline required.

A good modeling school will provide the basic information that is necessary and give the student a good idea of what it is like to be a professional model. Whereas most agents are quick to agree that the experience of a modeling school is not necessary, most photographers are grateful to see a model with experience and are not happy to find a model standing in front of their camera not knowing what to do. Agents maintain that testing will give the models the experience they require, but when they feel a new model is really hot, they will often send him out on bookings long before he is really ready.

There are a great many modeling schools around the country, and if you live in or near a moderately large city, there is apt to be one or more of them in your vicinity. Selecting a school (if you have a choice) is not an easy task. You will want to select a school that has a good reputation, is licensed by the state (if your state requires it) and has a knowledgeable faculty. You might be interested in knowing the experience of the staff and which of their students have gone on to successful careers. If a school is honest, they will answer all your questions and will not guarantee that they will make you a model but will give you the knowledge that you need to get started and will point you in the right direction. If you expect more than that, you are in the wrong place. Successful modeling is more than taking instruction, it's a combination of things, some of which can be learned, and some of which are you, like your personality and physicality. No one can teach you to be six feet tall or handsome. A school *can* show you how to work in front of the camera, and how to take advantage of your assets, however.

If, as a prospective model, you are living outside of one of the major modeling markets, you may find the only entrance to modeling is through attending a school. Basically, most schools provide courses that can be helpful. These generally include grooming, working in front of the camera, and putting together a portfolio. Most schools also have an agency as well and will try to get you work. Most of these school/agencies do not require you to take their classes in order to represent you if they feel they can get you work, but most prefer that you do take their classes.

There are many modeling school owners around the country who really do care about making professional models out of their students. The cold hard facts are that few will make it, as schooling alone will not make you a successful model. All the physical attributes must also be right, and a school can do nothing for you there. A school cannot afford to discriminate too much on who they take into their school. Many times they will sign up people who never can make it as fashion models, but if they only took on the ones who could really make it, they wouldn't have enough students to stay in business. There is nothing wrong with this as long as a school does not promise they can make a successful model out of you. No one can promise that. You are either right for it or you're not. Schooling can only take away the rough edges and better prepare you for what lies ahead.

Breaking into modeling through a modeling school can save a lot of grief and confusion. After taking the courses you should have a good idea of what the business is about and whether you want to pursue it as a career. This is not the cheapest way to get this knowledge, but it is probably the fastest and easiest, and undoubtedly, the most fun.

One of the best things that a modeling school has to offer is the modeling competition or convention. This is a money making enterprise for the schools, but attending one of these can be the best education you'll ever get. The bigger conventions (there are many of them) are held in New York, and the schools will bring as many students as they can for a week's worth of competitions, seminars (usually given by industry professionals) and a chance to meet the top agents who are there scouting for new faces. Some conventions are quite large with 1,000 or more students in attendance; some are small with under 50. The size is not as important as how many agents have been enticed to come. There are many small conventions in different parts of the country that take the time and effort to bring the agents to them, usually by assuming all of their expenses in order to do so. These local conventions may have all the benefits of the larger ones without costing as much since a hotel and air fare will not be necessary for the local student.

Attending a modeling school and one big convention in New York could easily set the student back $3,000 or more. Is it worth it? For students who have signed big modeling contracts at these conventions, the answer is undoubtedly a resounding "yes". For those who returned with nothing, the question might be harder to answer. Remember that ultimately the responsibility for a successful career lies with you alone.

Many working models have gone the modeling school route, although few want to admit to it. It seems it is better for the ego to say you were "discovered while walking down the street," or some such thing, but it really makes no difference. For some people, on the job training is enough, for others, reading a book such as this one is all they need. Others require the added opportunities that a school can give to help get them started. If you have the money and want to attend a modeling school, by all means do so. It could make things a lot easier for you to discover if you should really be in the business or not.

SECTION TWO

MODEL INTERVIEWS

Kyle Cody

Kyle Cody

I was born in Baton Rouge, Louisiana, and was 19 years old when I got started in modeling. I had one year of college at Louisiana State University before heading for Hawaii for the Summer to attend the University of Hawaii. It was at this time that I met a modeling agent, Kim Medeiros of the Central Island Agency in Honolulu. I only had two test pictures that weren't that great, but Kim saw potential in them and me. She was willing to represent me and help me with my career, but by the time I met her I was getting ready to leave Hawaii.

I didn't know anything about modeling, composites, test shots, photography sessions, go-sees - nothing. Kim advised me to move to a city that had some modeling opportunities and just jump in feet first. Since I have a sister who lives in Dallas, and I had already applied to Southern Methodist University and was accepted, I decided that would be the best place to go. I got accepted with an agency in Dallas as soon as I arrived in August of 1986. I decided to put off entering college until the following January so I could learn as much about modeling as I could. Kim had told me that it wasn't important at that stage whether I worked much or made a lot of money. It was most important that I learn how the business was run.

It was a good thing that I wasn't trying to earn a lot of money because I didn't work much. One of the reasons was the oil crunch had just hit and many businesses were adversely affected. The other reason was that I was too new, with no pictures, and my agency was also just starting and making their contacts. The odds were against me, but at only age nineteen, I felt I had plenty of time to learn the ropes. After four months there, I decided I'd learned as much as I was going to in Dallas and it was time to move on, so I went back to Baton Rouge. The following Summer I attended Harvard Summer School in Cambridge, Massachusetts and studied Macro Economics. I was accepted by The Hart Agency in Boston, and it was in Boston that I went on an open call for Wilhelmina Models. To my surprise they asked me to meet with the men's division in New York. The next day I was on a plane with a 10:00 appointment. The people at Wilhelmina were great. After I explained that I was leaving in one week to go back to Louisiana, they advised me to come back to New York in January. That is when they like to start "new faces." I thought I was dreaming. Here I was in Wilhelmina's booking room, discussing when the best time would be for me to move to New York! I was very excited.

Since I was in New York I decided to get some second opinions. I was curious to hear what the other agencies had to say. I went to Sue Charney's Faces without an appointment, and it took five minutes of persuading to get the receptionist to take my portfolio inside to the men's division. All of a sudden, I heard a woman with a French accent, and she was headed right toward me. This was Monique Corey. She took me into the booking room and introduced me to everyone. She said straight out, "I want to represent you." Before I knew it, I had a list of test photographers, a contract, and a list of apartments. She took my portfolio to have composites made. Everything was moving too fast. I was enthusiastic about Faces, because they were so willing to help me out, and Monique is a very kind lady for whom I have a lot of respect. Unfortunately, I did not have the money to move to New York. Without European tearsheets, I didn't feel I was ready.

Many people are confused about how New York agencies work. Parents and beginning models often think that the agencies will pay your airfare, rent and expenses. This just isn't

Kyle Cody's composite.

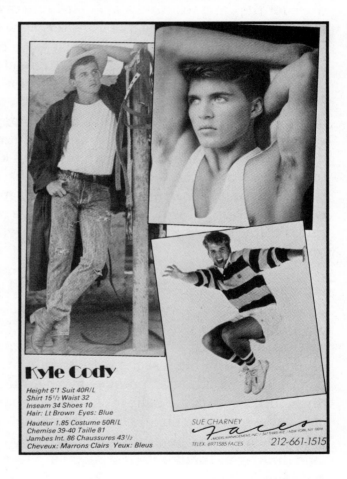

true. In some cases they may advance this money to you, but you must pay back every penny, which is usually deducted from your earnings. A working model is less of a risk, but a beginner may not earn any money for several months.

I returned to college in Baton Rouge for another semester then moved to Hawaii in January of 1988. I felt that in Hawaii, I knew people and I might get some work with the Japanese (who shoot a lot of work there) and possibly get a contract to go over to Japan and make a lot of money. While there, I did indeed work for the Japanese and started to build my portfolio. To help support myself, I also became a waiter. However, I didn't work as much as I thought I would because even the Japanese were looking for models with European tearsheets.

In April I decided to take a vacation in Europe during Spring Break. I contacted Monique at Faces who sent telexes to many agencies and my mini book to Glamour in Paris. I interviewed with Patrick at Glamour, and he offered to represent me if I moved to Paris for any length of time. I knew I would need to be there at least three or four months to obtain enough tearsheets, and I'd need to bring a lot of money to cover my expenses. Even if I worked right away, the agency would take up to 50% as their commission, leaving me with little to support myself.

I decided to move to Los Angeles instead. Here I am represented by SMASH. They are big enough to have established an excellent world-wide reputation, yet they are small enough to give me personalized attention. I'm also interested in getting into acting, which was another reason to relocate to L.A. I have started acting lessons with private coaches, and am now a member of SAG, which makes me feel more confident about my future auditions. I believe that all you need to do to succeed is to believe in yourself and have "killer" determination. You've got to follow through and go all the way. I'm glad I got into modeling even though it's not anything like what I thought it would be. It's not a glamorous job where you just get paid a lot of money; it's a lot of hard work and rejection. It's not the "rags to riches" type of story where you get signed up and instantly have it made. Anyone who is a model can tell you that.

Darren Coté

Darren Coté

I was restless in junior college in southern California, so when a girl I knew who was a model suggested that I get into modeling as well, I considered it. Between classes, I visited an agency and they expressed an interest in me right away. I had no conception of what the business was like, but I did think that it was unmanly. I had spent eight years playing football, and I didn't understand what modeling was all about. On my interview I was very relaxed, because I really didn't care what happened with it. I've found since then that being relaxed has helped me in this business. I never let the business get to me.

The agent took a couple of Polaroids of me, because I didn't have even one picture. He tacked one of them up on the wall, and as luck would have it, a European agent who was in town shortly thereafter saw it and wanted to hire me. Unfortunately, my agent had misplaced my file and couldn't remember my name or number. For one week, everyone was referring to me as "Paul Newman" because of my blue eyes. Finally, they found my file and contacted me. I was told that I was wanted in Milan either right away (this was October) or in January. I, being very naive, had no idea where Milan was, but it sounded far away and I thought it was probably in Northern California. That sounds pretty pathetic, but it's true. A few days later the agent called again saying that an agency in Paris was also interested, and I realized then they were talking about Europe, not the United States. I wasn't sure I wanted to go that far, but I was in class one day, I looked at the chalk board - I hadn't done my assignment for the day - and I knew right then, that would be my last day in class.

I did two days of testing in California and went to Milan, Italy, in January with just five pictures. Things were quite busy there even though I didn't work right away. The first thing I did was a press kit for Claude Montana, photographed by Bob Kreiger. For the first month and a half that I was in Europe, I traveled back and forth between Milan and Paris. At one point I was told to go to Paris for a page in Vogue, and for a model just starting out, this was Heaven. I was very excited when I went to Vogue's studio; click, click, click, they took two shots of me, and I walked out on Cloud Nine. When I saw the pictures in the magazine a couple of months later, they were small and the ugliest pictures I'd ever seen. I looked bad. It was such a let-down, I thought my career was over, but you go through that a lot when you're starting in the business. You don't know how to pace your emotions.

I ended up staying in Europe for seven months, and I worked quite a bit. I was what they called a "hard-core fashion model," very editorial. It wasn't glamorous, and I had to learn to do my own hair and makeup and take care of myself. I had never done any grooming, coming from a football background, and had to learn all that. I basically learned it from reading magazines and reading the little pamphlets that were enclosed in the products. The stress of the job alone is enough to cause your skin to break out. Even when your face is great, the strain will still show in your eyes. You have to remain confident and optimistic while still holding onto reality. I refer to that time in

Milan as "boot camp for modeling." Many other models referred to Milan as Vietnam. It was tough emotionally.

When I returned to California, I had a good book and a few thousand dollars, which was good. I had gone with only six

Darren Coté's composite.

hundred dollars and no ticket home, so I felt pretty good. I decided to head for New York and BAM! I was slammed in the face with the reality of just how tough and competitive this business really is. New York is the height of the market and I arrived in the Winter. I stayed for four months before a friend

of mine offered to drive me in a Rolls Royce back to California.
I went.

I decided to go to Tokyo, and was there for two months,
doing shows, print, and TV. It was great and that got me wound
up again. When I got back to California, I spent a year doing
other things, along with the modeling, so I wouldn't have to rely
on modeling alone. I worked in construction, real estate, and my
music. I got a booking for a German catalog, and it was fun, and
they told me I should go to Germany. I took them up on it and
went to Munich, without even contacting any agents there
before I arrived. I had a place to stay so I wasn't worried. I got
with an agency right away, and ended up staying for nine
months. I didn't speak German, but most of the people there
speak English so I had no problem. I got to do a lot of trips which
I enjoy, mostly for catalog work. I don't have much in the way
of pictures from all that, but it paid quite well. In between jobs
I kept busy with my music, and read the bible. You need to keep
yourself occupied, or otherwise the business can drive you
crazy. There are a lot of models who are walking a fine line and
they burn out.

I got involved with a church in Munich, and I spent nine
days in Romania doing a mission. That was an amazing thing
and one of the nicest things in my life. Life was so different in
Romania than in the United States. Their life was taken at a
much slower pace. In New York, I'm now involved with an
organization called Models For Christ. It's a support group for
models that has helped a lot of people. [See Resources section for
more information on this group].

I left Germany to go home for the Christmas holidays,
with every intention of going back, it was such a good experience
for me. I worked in Los Angeles for L.A. Models for a short time
when HV Models in New York called me and wanted me to work
for them. I wasn't planning to go to New York after my first
tough experience, but they really wanted me, so I thought I

would go try it. I really liked the people at HV, they're very nice, and I'm pleased to now be with this agency. I still work all over the world, but I'm now based in New York. I'm doing very well, especially since at this point of my life I'm getting into an older market, where there is more work.

I never finished college, and it only bothers me that I didn't finish for my parents sake. I know they would have liked me to finish. I might have missed the growing that happens in that environment, but I did a different growing. I grew up in a jungle; in Milan. That was enough growing up for me. I may go back to school one day to learn accounting or something. In the meantime, I'm an investor in my family's business. It's important for a model to invest his money for the future.

I think it's a good idea for a guy to finish school before starting to model, so he'll have something to fall back on. A guy can easily get started in modeling when he's in his mid-twenties, so he doesn't have to jump in it right from high school they way girls do.

I plan on staying in this business for a long time, because I'm doing well, it's a great education for me, and I'm enjoying it. Eventually, I want to sing, write, play the guitar or even produce, but that's in the more distant future. I'll probably continue modeling for another ten years. What's kept me together in this business and always positive is my relationship with Jesus Christ.

Cody Cupper

Cody Cupper

My very first glimpse of modeling, before I even thought about getting serious about the profession, was when I was selected as one of the top five finalists in a state-wide "Man Hunt" in Oregon. I was thrown in front of a live television camera and labeled a "hunk." I placed third and made off with a full-year scholarship to a local modeling school. But before I could even get off the set I was handed a message to call a producer who had just seen me on TV. My first day on the modeling scene and I'm already getting calls - Wow! I was skeptical, yes, but also very excited.

I met the producer that night at a restaurant where he bought me dinner and made arrangements to shoot pictures of me. Pictures were taken and he had visions of me in the movies right away. He advanced me a check for $1,000.00 to take with me while we traveled to various parts of the country. Airplanes and limousines were our means of transportation. Our main stop was New York where we spent a week or more meeting directors and local actors.

In the meantime, I had a couple of contacts back on the West Coast checking this guy out to make sure he was for real, because it was getting pretty deep.

He next offered me a movie role for $100,000.00 in which I would co-star with a couple of big name actors and actresses. I read the script and met the writer as well as the main actress. It all seemed legitimate; the high-life, first-class, exquisite hotels, limousines, New York, contracts, wining and dining. It was all happening for me only a week after a brief television appearance. How could it be real?

Well, actually it wasn't! The guy turned out to be a phony. Nothing that was supposed to happen was happening, and I got away before something bad *could* happen. I came to find out the truth about the guy, and it wasn't good. However, the good thing was I was $1,000.00 richer and learned a valuable lesson about the business of modeling.

You have to look out for the wierdos out there, because there are a lot of them! And no matter how real they might seem, you can never be too sure. So, for some advice to other beginning models: if you're a little skeptical about someone like that, ask your agent or someone to check on the guy. Chances are, if your agent has never heard of someone or can't find anything out about him, he's not worth talking to. He should talk directly with your agency rather than you anyway.

Since then, my career in modeling has been pretty ho-hum. I went through a year of modeling school and competed in New York at the annual IMTA Convention. It's been a lot of fun, but to be honest, I've put a lot more money into this business than I've gotten out of it - a lot more.

Unless you get a sincere big break and escalate in the modeling industry, it's going to take some dinero to get started. My suggestion is to go to college (which I am now doing) for an education and to find a profession you can work at for a steady income.

Besides being inconsistant, a career in modeling doesn't last forever. So unless you are very stable in the business, have another job to back it up, at least so you can pay the bills and still have enough money to continually build your book and become a familiar face in the modeling industry.

And remember, modeling is a profession. It's not all glamor; not at all. It's a lot of work, and a lot of money, so take it seriously and treat it like a profession. Most importantly, take good care of your biggest asset, your number one tool - your body. Daily exercise, a good diet, and a skin-care regimen should all be prerequisites and a routine for you. Good luck.

PHOTO BY FRANCESCO SCAVULLO

Michael Dupre

Michael Dupre

I was born in Chicago and raised in Eau Claire, Wisconsin.
I went to college at the Milwaukee School of Engineering.
After one year I met a girl who was in the modeling
business to a small extent and she introduced me to an agent
with Powers Model Management in Milwaukee. They set me up
with some photographers for testing and I hired a photographer
on my own for additional testing. I got together a good book for
Milwaukee and sent pictures to some New York Agencies. They
were all interested in me so I came to New York to see them, and
signed with Sue Charney. I did a couple of jobs in New York
before heading for Europe where I did very well.

In Europe I worked for Claude Montana, Versace, Armani, Valentino - everybody. I worked in Germany and Switzer-
land, where you can make a lot of money doing catalog. During
that time I came back to New York occasionally, but I basically
stayed in Europe for more than nine months developing my
portfolio and making money.

When I came back to New York, I decided I wanted to be
with a big agency so I signed with Ford Models. I stayed for a
year and half before switching to HV Models three years ago. I

left Ford because, even though I liked them and they liked me and I did very well, I felt they were a bit impersonal. They had too many models in relation to their staff. My needs were that I was working in many different markets, like Germany, L.A., Florida, etc., which is the best way to maximize your income, through many local agencies. Because Ford didn't make a commission on those jobs, they seemed to forget about me when I was gone and wouldn't promote me. Whenever I got back from a trip I would find that I didn't have any jobs, and I'd be doing nothing for a couple of weeks. HV is a much smaller agency and caters to my needs better.

I've been studying acting and I've done Soaps and a couple of Features besides modeling. I've had a lot of fun with the acting. I feel that I've gone about as far as I can with modeling, and I feel that I haven't been getting as much out of acting as I hoped to. My problem with acting was that 99.5% of all actors are unemployed, and I didn't want to bust my ass waiting for 10 years for the right part to come along. Now I only go out for the parts I'm right for.

While modeling I was also finishing my schooling by correspondence with an accredited school in California. I finished both my BA and my MBA. Thus prepared, I decided to get into the business end of modeling. I talked to the people at HV, and they hired me to become the director of public relations and scouting. It's going very well. I get to work with the new models, the young people, and since I've lived here for a while I can help them in a lot of ways getting adjusted to New York.

I still model for good clients, but basically I now work in the office from 9 to 6, and twice a month I travel to various cities in the United States and Europe, doing modeling conventions, scouting and giving seminars on modeling. I'm starting to organize an HV contest, a major model search every year with guaranteed contracts and prizes. I want HV Models to become one of the top agencies in New York.

My advice for models is to find the biggest market that you can that is near where you live. Go there and try to find an agency to work with. If you can't find an agency, now is the time to reconsider your options. Maybe you're not the right height, maybe you don't look the right way, maybe you should try acting

Michael Dupre's composite.

or something else. If an agency is interested in you, or they're not but you still think you have incredible potential, ask the agency for a list of their test photographers. Try to arrange a deal with the photographers so it doesn't cost you too much money, where you'll take some tests that will give you different looks like body shots, suit, head shots, jeans, etc. with both outside and inside locations. Try to get as good of a book as you can, and talk to the other models. Ask as many questions as you can.

Before you go to New York, send some pictures. If you can work there, they'll be able to tell from your pictures. You can even send in a simple snapshot before you've done anything. They can tell from that if you're right, even if your hair is wrong or everything is wrong. The only way to make money in this business is to go to Europe and New York, develop your book, become internationally known, then you can work anywhere and be a top model.

PHOTO BY FRANCESCO SCAVULLO

John Enos

John Enos

I started modeling in 1985 at age 23 in Boston. I had a girlfriend at the time who suggested that I get into it, but I knew absolutely nothing about it. I found a photographer in the yellow pages and tested with him. He charged me $135.00. They were the worst pictures I've ever done. The photographer was horrible; it was one of those rip-off type things. I took them to one agency in Boston and they turned me down, but the next agency I tried accepted me right away. My first job was for $110.00 an hour, but basically there is not much work for a male model in Boston. There are two big department stores there that book models, but if you work for one, you probably won't work for the other. I worked for Jordan Marsh, and I still do when I can.

I was sent over to a photographer named Bolling Powell to have some tests done. He was a good photographer in Boston who has since moved to New York and now shoots Vogue. He needed a guy to be with two girls, but he ended up just shooting me. When he saw my book, he said it was just horrible. He took an immediate liking to me and tested me the very next week for two days straight, with a stylist, hair, makeup, clothes - the works. He re-did my entire book. He sent my pictures to Elite Models in New York and Jan Gonet of the men's division flew up to Boston to see me. He thought I should go to Europe. I didn't have the money for that, and ended up selling my motorcycle. That together with the money from a two day booking in New York through Elite was enough for the trip. I told my mom and girl friend that I was going to Europe and travel around Italy. I packed up my skis, my ice skates; I took everything with me because I didn't know if I'd be working, but at least I could have some fun. I was going to be in the Alps, it was Winter, and I was going to ice skate, play some hockey, and do some skiing. Well, I ended up working a lot in Paris and Milan. I stayed over there for four months before returning to the United States. I worked for a while with Elite in New York, including a job with photographer Richard Avedon for Versace. I then returned to Europe for some shows that Summer.

When I again returned to New York I left Elite Models to join Wilhelmina. Although Elite had given me my first break, and I got along with everyone quite well, I felt that their men's division was not strong enough. I am very happy at Wilhelmina.

Being a model is tough. If you're working, it's fine, but if you're not it'll drive you nuts. When I first got to Wilhelmina it took a couple of months before I started to get bookings. When it gets slow you have to watch your pennies and be careful.

There are different markets to be aware of. Some models who don't work in New York work great in L.A. You won't make as much money there, but then it doesn't cost as much to live there. The same is true of Florida. In the Winter, the German's go down there and shoot all their catalogs. They are the catalog Kings. They sell everything by catalog, they're so organized. They'll book you for 10 days at $850.00 per day. That's $8,500.00 for less than two week's work. I like New York, although I'm not sure why. I don't like big cities; I'd much prefer to be on a farm somewhere.

I don't really know other male models and don't hang out with them. There's a couple of them that I like and can have fun with, but that's because they're not so pretentious. I mean, there are guys who have a complete library of every magazine they've ever been in and 10 portfolios, each one exactly the same, in addition to the ones that they have at the agency. They'll even

HEIGHT 6'1" SIZE 40L SHIRT 15½-34 WAIST 32 INSEAM 34
SHOES 11 HAIR BROWN EYES GREEN SAG

532-7715

John Enos' composite.

walk around in the Summer to go-sees wearing complete suits and ascots, and be completely made up. I laugh at that. I go in jeans and a tee shirt. Some people think that you should go to appointments in a tie. Some clients do want you to show up dressed up, but I think as long as you're clean and look okay that's enough. I think you should be yourself. My personality is a leather jacket and a tee shirt. An ascot just isn't me; that makes me laugh.

I'm friends with a lot of girls in the business, and that's because I prefer to be. I work with a lot of them - I'm lucky. I also work with men, but I get booked a lot to be a prop for the girls when they work for Vogue and campaigns like Anne Klein. Since everyone is focusing on the girls in those bookings, the pressure is off me and I can just be myself and have fun. I'm there to be a prop like a couch or a coffee table, so I don't have to try hard. These jobs often pay a lot so I like them.

The worst thing you can do in this business is to have an attitude like 'I won't do this and I won't do that.' I'll work with Scavullo or Avedon, but I'll also do a catalog for K-Mart; I don't care. I'm here to work and make money. I'm not here for the glamor. I don't even tell anyone that I'm a model. If I meet a girl on the street I'll tell her I'm a college student or a plumber. I don't think of modeling as an accomplishment; it's something that you either have or you don't. I don't brag about the jobs I get, or complain about them either. A lot of people rag on this business because they think it's the thing to do, but you've got to realize that we're paid a lot of money, and we get to travel and work with a lot of nice people. I prefer not to live in a big city, but I'm dealing with it. I have just enough in my apartment to survive. I could pick up tomorrow and move.

When I make enough money to be able to leave modeling comfortably, I'd like to do some real estate developing. I'd like to return to college and finish a degree in civil engineering. I like to work with my hands, I like to get dirty. I don't see myself behind a desk with a 9 to 5 job. For now I'm just taking it as it comes. I'll see what's going to happen.

Bill Gordon

Bill Gordon

I started modeling six years ago. A girlfriend of mine who was a model thought I should be one as well. I was living in Charlotte, North Carolina, at the time and she introduced me to a photographer there. It turned out that I was photogenic, and it worked out real well. I met another photographer and did more testing. I did not spend a lot on my pictures, and I don't think anyone should. The best thing to do is have a friend take pictures with a 35mm camera, which is what I did. It really doesn't take a lot of talent to take a simple picture. For the tests I bought clothes at the local department store and returned them afterward.

I took my portfolio to several agencies in Charlotte and worked with the Jan Thompson Agency there. Then I got a job as a flight attendant with an airline to support myself and allow me to travel cheaply. While on a trip to New York I met Zoli at a party at Xenon and started working with his agency. I relocated to New York at that time but I kept my airline job. There wasn't a lot of work for me because I looked too young. Although I was twenty-three, I looked much younger, and I just wasn't ready for New York. When Zoli died, a lot of models were let go and I moved to Florida, where I stayed and worked for two years. I did very well there before becoming a "gypsy model", spending time in many cities including Dallas, Houston and Atlanta. In order to work a lot, I found it necessary to go to many different markets.

A year and a half ago, I felt I was ready and moved back to New York. I went to several of the agencies, big and small, and signed with Faces. They did very well by me, but after a while, I felt I needed a change, and I recently switched to a new agency called Boss. They're a small agency, but they've got good clients. I would eventually like to be with a bigger agency, but my book doesn't have the right kind of tears yet. That's the name of the game now. Test shots are not enough. To be with a big agency, you've got to have great tears, because those will get you the best jobs. Fortunately, with the kind of clients that Boss has, my book doesn't have to be fabulous to get good jobs, it just has to be good. I'm about to have a new card made, and this one will be simple, but will include color, and it will cost under $900.00. People remember you from your card, so it's very important to have the best possible one you can.

Next Spring I plan to go to Europe to get some really good tearsheets. If I had gone a couple of years ago, I would probably be better off now, but every so often you come to a crossroads in your life and you have to make a decision about which way your career should go. I chose not to go to Europe at that point, when maybe I should have, but you never know. Things will work out fine though, I'm supporting myself, and have been for a couple of years.

Much of the work that I get is commercial modeling, and I find I can always get hired for it. I guess I've got the right look for it. Some of the best paying jobs that I currently get don't result in tearsheets because it's not print work. I work quite a bit doing showroom modeling, and I also have many clients who use me as a fit model. Both of these categories require you to be the right size to fit the clothes, fit modeling in particular. To be a fit model, you must be a perfect 40 Regular with a 32 inch waist, a 33 inch inseam, a 15 1/2 neck and a 33 sleeve. You should also be just six feet tall, because any taller would require

Height 6'1"
Size 40R
Shirt 15½-33
Waist 32
Inseam 33
Shoes 10½
Hair Brown
Eyes Blue

Bill Gordon's composite.

a long jacket rather than a regular. With fit modeling, the prototype clothes are actually sized to you, and made according to what looks good on *you*. I have to spend a lot of time at the gym to stay my exact same size, being careful not to get *too* bulky. Many people don't know too much about doing showroom or fit modeling, but you can make $70,000.00 a year doing that kind of work if you have enough regular clients. If I never make it as a print model, there is a lot of other modeling work that I can do and still make a good living.

The key thing to working as a model is networking with other people. I socialize a lot and many of my friends are other models or clients. I get a lot of referrals that way, and I find that a client will pay more attention to you if you were recommended by someone he knows. If they like you, they are apt to use you.

Although I plan to keep modeling for a long time, I plan to eventually get into acting. I think I'll do well in that field.

PHOTO BY AARON WARKOV

Jesse Harris

Jesse Harris

I was cajoled into modeling by a friend of mine; it was not something that I wanted to do at first. I was driving cars for a car leasing company in Los Angeles. My friend kept after me to model and practically drove me over to a photographer's to get some pictures done. She was much more determined than I was. My interest was first sparked when she showed me a GQ, and I thought that wasn't too hard. I found out different later. I didn't do anything with those pictures that she had talked me into doing for three or four months. I met the actress Tina Louise, who introduced me to her manager, who knew someone at Mary Webb Davis Agency in L.A.

I was told at the agency that the pictures I had weren't good enough and I was much too tall at 6'3". They took me on anyway, and threw a list of test photographers at me. I called every one, but a lot of those photographers didn't do testing and they hung up on me. Even as I was getting tests, for four months they didn't send me out on any go-sees. A new booker came in and he started to send me out and I got a few bookings right away for catalog and a couple of shows. I still had my day job, and had worked my way up through the mail room and into the computer department. I had wanted to be a Fireman, but my eyesight was not good enough.

After a while I decided I needed to go to Europe to get tearsheets. I was starting to get more work and I felt I was ready. I quit my day job, and as fate would have it, I didn't work any more as a model for the next two months. I had to get a job as a waiter. I met an agent named Luigi from Fashion Model in Milan. He said he wanted me, but not just yet. I was very anxious to go so I kept sending him my pictures, and he kept saying the time wasn't right. A Paris agency said the same thing. Finally an Agency in Germany said to come over, and I went before they could change their mind. I got enough work there to support myself and actually come out a little ahead. I stayed in Germany for three months, before calling Luigi again and he still said not yet. I figured there was never going to be a right time so I went anyway. When I showed up at Fashion Model, he wouldn't take me on, so I went to Beatrice and they took me. Unfortunately, I only got one job with them, so I switched to Model Plan, where I didn't do much better at first.

Before too long, I started to get some good testing. After three months in Italy, I went to Paris and worked a little there. I got a great job for a Japanese client that was shot in Morocco, and they paid me about $4,000.00 in cash. I couldn't open a bank account in Paris, so I stashed the money in my hotel room. My room was broken into, and my money was stolen. Fortunately, they didn't take my book, although from that day on I didn't get another booking in Paris. I went back to Milan, and I finally started to work more regularly. By that time I had been in Europe for a year. Altogether I ended up staying in Europe for almost three years, and did fairly well, working almost every day. Most guys don't stay that long to get their tearsheets, but it takes some people longer than others. I finally decided to come back to the United States to further my career.

The Zoli Agency had scouted me in Milan, and I had agreed to sign with them when I got to New York. I've now been based in New York for over two years, but I've gone back to Europe for assignments on many occasions. I'd like to model for at least a couple more years, but I have no idea of what I'll do in the future. I've made no plans, although I do have a few hobbies that maybe could earn me a living. I like photography, but I wouldn't want to be a fashion photographer. I'm trying not to think about the future because it's scary. I keep myself busy so I don't have time to think about it.

*Jesse Harris'
composite.*

If you want to be a model, you have to be focused and persistent. When I first started I was very introverted, but being outgoing is very important. It's not only your personality on the set, but on the go-see as well. You have to be personable, but you can't seem to be kissing ass either. It's a fine line to tread, because people are constantly judging you. If a client doesn't like you, he won't hire you.

You should have something else in mind that you can do after you've finished with your modeling career, however short or long that is. I wish that I had something to fall back on, but I couldn't do just anything. You get used to a certain level of living, and the flexibility of working freelance. You can't have that freedom in just any job.

PHOTO BY NOEL SUTHERLAND

Carl Holmes

Carl Holmes

I was introduced to modeling by a friend of mine who was a photographer and a model in South Carolina. He told me about the Millie Lewis agency in Columbia, which was about an hour away from where I was working and going to school. He explained that it would be a hobby because there wasn't much money involved, but it would be good experience. Every year Millie Lewis holds a convention where agencies from New York, Paris, and all over the world would come to scout for new talent. I signed up for modeling courses that taught me how to build a book, go on interviews, do runway, etc. Because it was a long commute for me, I went mainly on the weekend. I did a few local commercials through the agency, as well as some print work, that paid my traveling expenses and for the modeling courses, with some extra left over. Of course, the rates in South Carolina don't compare with the rates in New York. It was a great learning experience.

From there I went on to the convention, and I won best overall for men. Different agencies approached me, that were interested. One of them even gave me airline tickets to come up to New York which is unusual. The following week I handed in my notice at work, and the next month I was on my way to New

York. Modeling was always something that I had dreamed about, and now I was on my way. I thought if I didn't find out now about it, I'd always be wondering "what if?"

I was with Legends in New York, but I didn't sign with them right away. This turned out to be lucky because they were not a good agency. They just threw me out there with no guidance. Modeling in New York is definitely not like modeling in Columbia, South Carolina, although my training certainly helped me. After a couple of months of no testing I switched to Kay Models which was better. They sent me out testing to build my book, and gain camera experience which is vital. Then they sent me out for work assignments, and I got a few jobs that yielded some tearsheets. From Kay Models I switched to a larger agency, HV Models, which was a step up. There I started to do larger jobs that were higher paying. I was twenty-five at this point and just old enough to get cigarette and liquor ads. Previously, I was photographing so young that it was difficult to get work. There was too much competition in that age group. At twenty-five, I began to get a little more character in my face. I also started to get catalog work, that you need to stay alive in this business. I finally was able to support myself in modeling. When I first got to New York I had a variety of part-time jobs to help pay the bills. The market for black models is much smaller with even more competition, then it is for my white colleagues. It's important to zero in on your market, build your book on it, and go out and get the work. Your attitude is important. You get turned down a lot, but a client doesn't care what terrible thing happened to you yesterday. They don't want to see a frown. Modeling is like a marathon, not a hundred yard dash. You've got to stay persistent, stay positive, pound the pavement and stay on top of it. You can never get relaxed, and think it will stay the way it is. There is always someone new getting into the business who is going to be working just as hard as you are. You can't just rely on your agent, you've got to pull for yourself as well.

I never went to Europe, and I was fortunate enough to get some tearsheets right here. Lately however, I've been thinking about making the trip. I know I'd get better tearsheets that would get me better work here. You're only as good as your book; it's like a resume, and it needs to be constantly up-dated.

Carl Holmes' composite.

Just recently, I switched agencies again to Zoli, who has the best clients. I'm also getting into TV, and they have a TV department to help me. I finally feel that I'm a model who made it. I made it through the ups and downs, and it's good now. The future looks good, and I plan on doing it until I can't do it anymore. I'm not pursuing an acting career, because I'm making a comfortable living as a model and it's getting better every year. My wife is a clothing designer, and we hope to open a boutique together soon. If it does well, we hope to grow into a franchise. It's a risky business, so we're starting off small.

I think you should make sure that you get your education before thinking about a modeling career. You'll need to have something to fall back on. In this business nothing is guaranteed from one day to the next. You always need to have somewhere to go, and have something there that you can do.

PHOTO BY MICHAEL LOUIS

Chris John

Chris John

I started out locally in Buffalo, New York. I thought if Jim Palmer could be a model, then it was okay for me to do it. Two years ago, I went with my parents to London for an extended vacation, and while there I contacted some agencies there. I had brought my pictures from Buffalo, and got accepted by Askew Team agency after being turned down by quite a few others. I started to do some testing, and I was very fortunate to get some commercials, since I had no experience. I also did a little catalog work. I stayed for about two and a half months, before heading off for Milan. I had sent some tearsheets sent ahead by my agency, and I was refused. I thought the tears that had been sent were terrible, so I sent some myself that I liked better, and was accepted by My Models. They weren't the best agency, but I didn't think that should matter. I was at a great disadvantage, because I didn't bring much money with me. That's the big mistake that a lot of people make. You have to have money, because the work you get there doesn't pay much to begin with, and your agency takes half of it. You need to put in a lot of time before you get anything unless you're lucky. So I didn't have any money for a while, and got behind in my rent. I was rooming with three other people in one room, and sharing a bathroom with eight or nine other people. I never want to do that again.

I managed to get some tearsheets, but the whole situation was very difficult. I had a tendency to gain weight because I was bored and unhappy. My girlfriend was back home, and we had been together for a while which made our separation difficult. It was also getting close to Summer and my friends were going to return from their first or second year at college and I wanted to be with them.

When I came to New York, I went to a couple of agencies, and I don't know if I came at the wrong time or they just didn't like my look, but they didn't want me. I finally got with a smaller agency. I was there for about a year, on and off, but 1988 was a turbulent year for me. My mother was sick during this time and I was home for a month and a half with her. I also had an accident on my bicycle; I was riding with no helmet on and my Walkman cranked up. A car pulled out in front of me while I was going about thirty miles an hour, and I jammed on the brakes. The bike stopped, but I didn't. I went flying over the handlebars, and the bike landed on top of me. I fractured both my arms, and I went home to Buffalo to recuperate. I'm better now, but there was a terrible scrape on my face that worried me. Fortunately, you can't see it now.

While I was home, I thought a lot about my modeling career. Things had just started getting rolling before my accident. I had just done a Caribbean trip and had been to Brazil for Brazilian Vogue, which gave me some good tears. At the time of my accident I was booked for several jobs that had to be cancelled. These would have earned me seven or eight thousand dollars.

I've only been back modeling for a short time, and I just switched agencies to Zoli. I felt that being with a larger agency could help my career. I thought I had gone as far as I could with the agency I was with. I feel very comfortable with Zoli; I think they're the best men's agency in New York.

Right now I'm not sure about the future. I don't like the idea of a nine to five job, I like to have the freedom to do what I want. I like to go running, or take time off to visit my family. I still have to work hard; it isn't as easy as everyone thinks it is.

Chris John's composite.

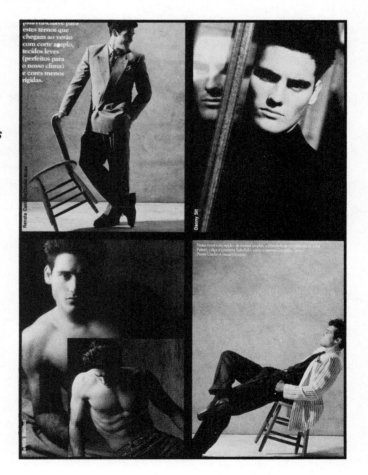

I'd like to go back to school soon and get my associates degree in business; I only need a few more credits. I'm doing some commercials now, but I'm not one of those people who wants to be a starving actor. I'd like to make enough money modeling so

I can invest in my own business. I'd like to be able to open a place in Clearwater, Florida, that will serve Buffalo Chicken Wings, a popular dish in Buffalo, New York. I'm a very good cook.

I haven't spent too much time in Florida, but it's very friendly, peaceful and relaxed. I still don't feel too at home in New York City. It's still a little too crazy here, and since I don't have a car I can't get out into the country. New York isn't my place.

You have to be realistic about your modeling career. You should get a few opinions from some other people in the business, and try to get as honest an answer as you can. Quite often people will lie to you because they don't want to hurt your feelings. But don't ever let anyone stop you. You have to do what you want. Everyone gets turned down at one time or another. If you keep on pushing, you'll hopefully get into it. At the same time, you have to be realistic. If you're working very hard and nothing is happening, then maybe you should get into something else.

Stan Newman

Stan Newman

I studied business and art education in college. After graduating I wondered how I could possibly pay off my student loans on a teacher's salary of $12,000.00 per year. I couldn't imagine that being my lifestyle. So, I got into international marketing for Revlon. While on a business trip in Paris I met Zoli, one thing led to another, and he introduced me to Glamour who said that I should be a model. I had a nine to five job and I wasn't interested in becoming a model, but they prevailed upon me to take a couple of pictures, which I did. About four days later, Glamour called me and asked me if I wanted to shoot a commercial for Pepsi in Spain. I hesitated until they told me my salary would be more than I earned in a year at Revlon. I accepted. After that, I never left modeling, and I spent the next two and a half years in Paris.

I was very fortunate to work every day, traveling all over Europe on trips for two weeks, three weeks, even a month at a time. It was a wonderful experience. Most of that work was for catalog, which paid very well. While in Italy, I got into the music business and cut three records. I met very nice people who got me into it, and they even put me on TV. It was great, but after two and half years, I was ready to go back to the United States and speak English again. My social life was the pits because my

French and Italian were not good. My vocabulary didn't extend much beyond baby talk - oui, oui, non, non, si, si. After a while it just wasn't for me, and by this time I had plenty of tearsheets in my portfolio to get me work in the States.

When I returned, I signed with Zoli and work was okay and I made a good living. But Zoli died around 1980, and the agency was in a bit of a turmoil. I got nervous and moved over to Wilhelmina. It was good, I can't complain, but during the course of years in New York one has to work very hard. Modeling anywhere else in the world, it's very easy to become successful. In New York you have to be extremely professional, you have to be on top of things, you need to be a lawyer and an accountant, and always be very aware of your health. I did mostly commercial print ads like Maxwell House, Burger King, and Continental Airlines. I wasn't doing the fashion things like Gianni Versace or Armani; I was always doing the goody two-shoes things, but they paid good money.

Before long I realized that for longevity for myself, and to maximize my income, I should be strictly in the commercial field. Not everyone can do it, because you have to be very all-American and marketable. I was very fortunate to fall in that realm, so I went with a commercial agency, McDonald/Richards, which has been great for me. They push me, they believe in me, and they're very nice to their clients. I'm also with the Johnson Agency in Greenwich, Connecticut, that gets me quite a bit of work.

With modeling these days you have to find where your niche is. If you have a great body, you'll end up doing a lot of work-out things; if you're thin and look great in suits, then that's what you'll do. What I'm trying to do is get myself very resort, all-American healthy, every-day-next-door-guy. That seems to be working.

I'm currently putting together a new composite, which I do twice a year. Clients always want to see more, better, and newer stuff. This time there's going to be color in it, and that's very expensive. It will probably cost about $3,000.00 for 1,000 of them, and that's a fairly low price. But an up-to-date card is necessary, because many clients no longer look at your portfolio.

Height 6'0   Inseam 33
Suit 40R   Shoes 10½
Shirt 15½/33   Hair: Dk Blond   SAG
Waist 31-32   Eyes: Blue   ALL SPORTS

McDONALD/RICHARDS, INC.
156 FIFTH AVENUE NEW YORK, NEW YORK 10010
212/627-3100

Stan Newman's composite.

They don't have time. They want to see what they want to see in your composite and the Polaroid that they shoot. If they don't see it in your composite or the Polaroid, you don't get the job.

There are other things that can give you an edge. I find out from my agent what the client is looking for and dress accordingly. If they are looking for a suit, or shorts, or a tee shirt, that's what I'll wear. If I don't, I don't get the job, it's as easy as that. Basically, clients don't have much of an imagination, but it's often not enough to just look the part. If they want someone who is 30 years old (I'm 31) and from California, then that's what I am that day. You have to tell them what they want to hear, even if you have to lie a little. It acts as a selling point. After seeing so many people, the client often loses his objectivity and can be confused. When you walk through the door, you have to make a statement, whatever that may be, and they'll either want you or they won't. You either win or lose.

With commercial modeling, the older you become, the more distinguished and the more mature you become, the better the market. There's a lot more work out there for a older gentleman. Then you're dealing with someone who *can* have kids and a wife. Or you can do an ad with a Porsche and be believable. I mean a 25 year old kid can't have a Porsche unless someone gave it to him. But someone in their late 30's or 40's with one is realistic and can sell the cars to the proper age group. The same is true with Rolex watches, cashmere jackets or $2,500.00 suits. Upscale merchandise of that type requires an older model.

I've already begun plans for what I'll do after modeling, although I can probably work for as long as I want to. I'm investing money in real estate and I bought some property with a friend of mine in St. John, U.S. Virgin Islands, and we will build a very small resort. Hopefully, through my contacts in the business, I can use this resort for location work.

Campion Platt

Campion Platt

I first started modeling when I came to the city from a school in Michigan to study at the Institute of Architecture and Urban Studies. People told me that I should look into modeling, and someone sent me up to see Antonio Lopez, a famous illustrator, who died a few years ago. Antonio asked me if I had any photos, and all I had was the photo on my drivers license. He sent me over to Barry McKinley to have some photos taken, who is a very big photographer. Barry also asked to see my photos, and I showed him my license. He said that was good enough, and booked me the next day for a shooting with GQ.

I wasn't with an agency, and we had quite a bit of confusion over signing the voucher. Coming from a business background, I didn't want to sign anything unless I knew exactly what it was about. I was finally convinced in no uncertain terms that it was no big deal to sign a voucher. So I went ahead and signed it. The next day, Barry McKinley booked me again for a trip for Italian Vogue in Florida. It was for the same week that I was supposed to take my entry exams for graduate school, because I was applying to Columbia. So in my first week shooting with Barry McKinley, I upset him when I had to leave the shooting in the morning to rent a car and drive to Miami University to take my exams. I did return for the rest of the shooting in the afternoon.

When I returned to New York, I asked Barry to suggest an agency for me, and he told me about several. After two or three days I decided that Zoli would be the best for me. I knew that I could make a lot of money modeling, but I still wanted to be able to go to school. I had heard some sordid tales about the industry. Even today, people think that all male models are gay. Of course, that's not true. I thought Zoli men were very classic, and the kind of model that I was too. As it turns out, I do a great deal of black tie, suits, classic all-American. I was with Zoli for about seven years. After Zoli died, things changed at the agency, and I felt that Vicky Pribble, my booker, was getting farther away from the board and more into management. The connection between you and your booker and the clients is probably the most important aspect of the business. I think that many people don't understand that. Your booker is paramount to your success. You can have a great look and suffer immeasurably because you don't have someone who's interested in pushing you, or you don't have a good relationship with. After a while, I decided to switch agencies, and I'm now with HV Models.

I had finished by schooling during this time and had worked in the business of architecture full-time for three years. Fortunately, my office was right near the heart of the Photo District, so I would often take a long lunch to do a booking. Because I managed the office, it wasn't too hard to arrange my schedule to permit this. It was rather interesting to switch gears during the day to start in the office in the morning yelling at contractors, speaking to clients, attempting to get jobs, and drafting, and shift gears and put on black tie, smooch with a girl and drink some champaign, and have some lunch before returning to the office to finish out the day. Those brief modeling assignments paid more than I'd make in a week and a half in the office. So for the last seven years, I've been living a dual life, and I plan to continue that way.

I spent a little time in Milan, but I didn't get too much editorial work. Instead I got mostly ads that were good paying jobs. Later on I went to Paris and the same thing happened again. Most models go over there for tearsheets to build their book, but since that doesn't seem to happen for me, I've found that I always work better in this country. That's fortunate because, aside from brief trips, I prefer working here.

Campion Platt's composite.

The business has changed a great deal since I began. First of all in sheer numbers of models and agencies. The client base is probably just the same or maybe even gotten smaller. There's not the same amount of work out there for a model as there used to be. Of course, I've never thought of modeling as something to sustain your life on. In fact most of the older models I know are sorry that they weren't getting into some other profession. As a model you rarely work every day. You don't have the same kind of life as a woman who is a model. As businesses go, it's probably one of the few that's discriminated the other way, in terms of the rate structures, the amount of time that you work, and the pampering and everything else that goes on. I would advocate that everyone who gets into the business has some other serious intention besides just modeling.

For the future, I will continue to model. Over the years I've established clients who will continue to use me. I love the travel, which is always fun. I love to get out of the city and get paid two thousand dollars to sit on a beach. It's well worth your while. I have my own practice in architecture now and my time is very important to me. I make it very clear to my agency that I'm still willing to do jobs, but I need a good deal of notice to arrange my schedule.

It takes a certain mentality to work in this business. If you're a male model, you're probably going to be starting at the age of nineteen or twenty or so. At that age you're not as outgoing, you're still introverted at that age, still finding out what the world is about. You have to be extroverted enough to go out and promote yourself. You can't sit home, because you need to get out and see your clients. It's balancing the reality of the job which is basically that you are being hired for your look rather than your personality. That has some intrinsic problems, because most relationships that you cultivate in your life with family or friends is based more upon your personality and character than how you look. It's important to balance the two.

PHOTO BY BRUCE WEBER FOR CALVIN KLEIN MENSWEAR

Rob Simonson

Rob Simonson

I started modeling in Idaho which has a very small market, at the age of twenty-six. I was a late bloomer, but because my look is classic, my age helped me. I did a show in Idaho before moving to Los Angeles. I approached the agencies in L.A. which is probably the most difficult part of the whole deal. A lot of the agencies aren't interested in you if you have no pictures, but how do you get them? I only had a few pictures that my girlfriend had taken, but those were enough to get me accepted with the Vaughn Agency. From there I did a lot more testing which provided better shots. It was sort of a snowball effect. The more you do, the more you're able to do. You have to grow a bit before you'll get any jobs. I was a marketing major in college, and I've found that the skills I learned have helped me tremendously in modeling.

I gave myself a time limit and a certain amount of money to invest in my modeling career. If nothing happened before then, I was going to stop. It got really close to that, because I was running out of money. I was almost ready to give it all up when I was fortunate enough to get a Calvin Klein campaign that was being shot in New York by Bruce Weber. I flew into New York for the booking that involved several other models and a couple of days. That ad went national, but they only ended up using one model's pictures, mine. This was a break for me, because it was a very big campaign, and it was also their last menswear campaign.

With those tears I went to Europe, which is a typical place for a model to go to get more tears. You can good artistic jobs there because the magazines seem more at ease with allowing the photographers to use their style. I stayed there for about ten months, living in Paris and frequently traveling to Milan. It's all part of the evolutionary process of becoming a model.

I returned to New York two years ago, joined Zoli, and have been based here ever since. Zoli had scouted me in Los Angeles, and many other models from Vaughn also went with Zoli when they came to New York. In the past year Zoli has gone through a major transition. Their head booker was replaced, which is a very traumatic thing to happen for a model. The agency is your backbone and when someone is working with you and for you as an agent/client relationship always is, you rely on them. Most of the models were a bit afraid of what would happen, but it worked out very well. I think that Zoli has the best men's agency in town right now. I'm very happy there, and everyone has been very nice to me. Some people get upset with their agents and snap at them, but I think it's very important to apologize if you do that. This is a relationship that you need to keep. It's certainly not beneath me to apologize, especially when I'm wrong, which happens. It happens to everyone.

I do a lot of modeling with suits. I'm a Forty Regular, which is just the right size for it. My look is sort of European classic that's not so European as to be strange to American catalogs. I have the best of a few worlds. The catalog clients are important, because they're regular business. I also do many advertising campaigns. I admit to having some difficulty with cigarette and liquor ads. I don't think people should smoke or drink, but it's part of the business to advertise those products. They pay enormous amounts of money, that's hard to turn down. I let the clients know that I don't smoke, and I won't inhale it. It would make me sick. It's not good for your career to refuse these ads, though.

Rob Simonson's composite.

HEIGHT: 6' / SIZE: 40 R / WAIST: 31 / INSEAM: 33 / SHIRT: 15½-34 / SHOE: 10 / HAIR: Brown / EYES: Blue-Green

ZOLI
(212) 758 6611

model team
Sonja Ekvall
Arbeitsvermittlung von Fotomodellen
im Auftrag Der Bundesanstalt Für Arbeit
Schlüterstraße 60
2000 Hamburg 13
Telefon (040) 41 41 03-0
Telex 211101 movie d

bananas
42 89 42 09

WHYNOT UOMO
PRINT & SHOW

The business has been good for me, and I have no complaints. I've been able to be myself, and I'm basically my own boss. I probably wouldn't be a good actor, because I don't see myself changing my character to be someone else. I've put three years into modeling so far, if I put a couple more into it, I'll probably stay in it. It depends on the economy which definitely affects the fashion industry.

In the future I would like to stay in this industry, but if not, it's certainly let me acquire quite a bit of knowledge. I probably couldn't earn the kind of money that I make as a model. It's a great opportunity for a guy my age - I'm twenty-nine - to save some money. I know how to work, so I'm not afraid of the future. Many models are afraid of the future, rather than happy about it. They think they won't be able to do anything else. Everyone can do something else. I worked on landscaping before I was a model, and I'm sure that if I learned a little more about it, I could have my own landscaping or contracting business if necessary. I've worked since I was twelve; I painted houses and cut lawns. Whatever the future brings, I'm not worried. There's a value to your time, and you've got to use it to make money. As long as you give people what they want, they'll hire you. If you do your job, and you do it well, sometimes good things come your way. Knock on wood. *Always* knock on wood when you say things like that.

Brian Solano

Brian Solano

I started modeling in January 1987. I was playing baseball at the University of Florida, hurt my shoulder, and had surgery on it. I transferred home to Tampa to Hillsborough Community College. I love baseball and gave it another try, but my shoulder continued to give me problems.

Instead, I involved myself in student government. I went to a Republican Party meeting one night and met an advertising agent who told me I should get into modeling. She set up a meeting with a photographer, and after taking some pictures, he sent me to a modeling agency. Unfortunately, I never got any work from that agency because I didn't know what I was supposed to do. They gave me a go-see list and I didn't even know what it was. I was basically naive about the whole modeling profession.

After a month I signed with another agent, Wendy Davis of Model Talent Management, and that's when I started to work. Wendy really loved my look and encouraged me. She helped me put a portfolio together (I hadn't known what that was either) which was expensive, but necessary, and sent me out on go-sees. I got almost every job I went out for. I started doing fashion shows and print work that gave me confidence in front of the camera.

I made many contacts at the International Modeling & Talent Competition that I attended in Orlando, Florida, in the Spring of 1987. These included agents from Europe, Los Angeles and New York. Before I made use of any of these contacts, however, I finished out my semester at college. I did continue modeling in the Tampa area while waiting to go to Paris for the Glamour Agency there. I was able to head for Europe in June of 1987 and my first stop was Paris.

That first day I sat around the agency with terrible jet-lag while everyone was deciding how they should mold my career. After a couple of days, I had some testings set up which turned out very well and were a surprise to everyone. I was up for several jobs right away and got a commercial in the very first week. After that it was more testing and more go-sees. At the end of June an agency from Milan, Italy, came up to Paris and saw me.

A week later I was flying to Milan to spend some time with Beatrice Models. They put me up in a hotel and I didn't speak a word of Italian. I was just beginning to understand a little French! I felt lost and alone, but I knew I had to stick it out if I expected a career in this business. The next afternoon I was given four appointments: Giorgio Armani, Moda magazine, Mondo L'Uomo, and Sclavi studio. I got lost on the Metro, so I took expensive cabs instead. All of these interviews went well I thought. One of them even told me I was *too* good looking for the job! The result of these first go-sees was a three-day booking for a Giorgio Armani show in Rome.

Although the Summer is very slow in Europe, I was able to work several times and actually made a little money. After spending a month in Italy, I returned to Paris and worked for Levi's, German catalogs, and the collections. The collections go-sees were all packed into a two or three day period so it was very hectic and the competition was tough. I think every top model in the world was there competing for a very few jobs. I got call backs from about 75% of my go-sees, which was very lucky, since at that point I hardly had any pictures to show at all. At the call backs they wanted to see everyone walk, something I frankly did not have much experience at.

Brian Solano's composite.

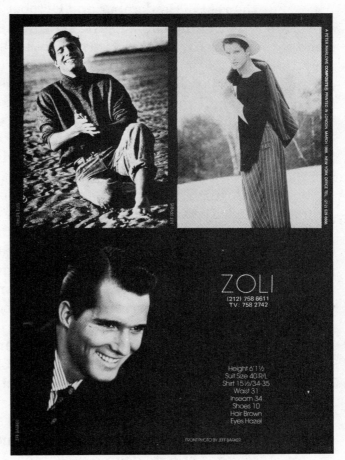

I was very fortunate to get booked for two shows, Claude Montana and Angelo Tarlazzi. While I was watching another show that a friend was booked for that I didn't get, I was **approached by an editor of British Vogue magazine who was**

also in the audience. He said he thought I had the right look for a one week shooting in Aruba. I tried to act cool, but inside I was overwhelmed. I was skeptical that it was too good to be true, but they did put a hold on my time for November.

For the rest of September and October it was very slow, and although I was on hold for several campaigns, none of them came through. In November, I was off to Aruba. The work was very difficult, up in the morning at six and working until midnight every day. I also had a stomach virus, but I tried to be fun to be around. It was part of learning to become professional. You've got to appear to be having a great time, even when you're not. The shooting turned out to be a success, and I was put on hold for another shooting to be done in mid-May in Vienna, Austria.

After Aruba I went home to Florida for December and January to be with my family. In late January I came up to New York and was signed with Zoli and did a promotional piece for them. While they worked on putting my tears together and making a new composite, I returned to Florida once again to prepare to move to New York. At the end of March 1988, I moved up to New York, and Zoli arranged living accommodations for me. I worked several jobs, including Saks Fifth Avenue. The British Vogue job in Austria came through and I left for that. While in Europe I was convinced to go to London and got enough bookings to stay there for quite a while and actually made some money.

After returning to New York, I wasn't sure whether I wanted to continue modeling or not so I returned home to finish out my Associates of Arts degree in Tampa. While back home I've continued modeling, and it's a lot easier and more relaxed here. I've been working with the Irene Marie Agency in Ft. Lauderdale, and many big clients come down here to shoot. It's a much healthier environment. When I get my degree, I'll return to New York for awhile and see how I like it. I'm not sure

I'll stay in modeling. Perhaps I'll move on to acting or join the family business.

Along the way I have been filled with self-doubt and insecurity. I guess a model has to deal with all of that every day as you grow and gradually gain confidence, and discover your limitations. I don't want to try to become someone else. I just want to be Brian Solano. I think that's important.

PHOTO BY STEVE AUCOIN

Tom Tripodi

Tom Tripodi

I grew up in New York and finished my last two years of college in Hawaii. After graduating I stayed there and worked in real estate and time shares. I was able to fly for free, so I used to come to New York every three weeks or so to visit with my friends. A friend of mine had an Uncle who was an art director for Avon, and I was introduced. He asked me if I was interested in modeling and I said 'sure.' He told me that the next time I was in New York to see him and he'd arrange a test. I didn't have a clue as to what a test was, but I agreed.

The test that was set up was with some top girls, and I was starstruck. The test turned out well, and I was told I had possibilities, but I should go to Europe. Because I could fly for free, I decided to go with my girlfriend for a three-day weekend to Rome. I was given three names of agencies in Milan: Fashion Models, Model Plan, and Beatrice. I called them up to set up an appointment, and told them that I was with Zoli in New York for the last year, and they told me to contact them. This wasn't true, but I thought it would help. I went up to Milan and my girlfriend returned home with all the luggage. I was to follow one day later. I showed the agencies the few pictures that I had and they sent me out immediately for some shows. I didn't speak any

Italian, and they sent someone along with me to interpret. I got four shows, and stayed to do them. They worked out well, so when I returned to Hawaii, I sold my car and rented out the houses I owned and determined to go back to Milan. When I called Milan, they said it was slow, and not a good time to return, so I went to New York to see Zoli. I went dressed in a three-piece suit with these horrible, horrible shoes, my hair was long and parted in the middle, and being a salesmen in time shares I was wearing all this gold jewelry. Zoli said "Well, Tom, I think you need to go to Europe." I told him I had just been there, and wanted to work in New York, but he said I needed a lot more tearsheets to be able to do that.

I called up Italy and said I was coming, and they again told me it was very slow and not a good time. I was determined and had some money, so I went anyway and was represented by Fashion Models. The head of the agency said I would never make it, but one of the bookers there, Mary Stella, really liked me, and pushed me. It was very slow, but they managed to get me one job. I was expecting tuxedos, but I was dressed up like a grease monkey for a gasoline company. My first tearsheet resulted from that, a little thing about six inches big. It was funny, but horrible. I thought that now that I had a tear, I would immediately get a lot of work, which didn't happen. I did get a couple of other jobs. One of them was a two-day booking out of town for a commercial. After the first day I got home very late to a message saying I needed to call GQ. It was so late, I didn't call, and the next day I had to catch a five a.m. train to finish my commercial. I called my agent who thought I was crazy not to return the call and she called them. It turned out it was for a go-see in Rome, which was a seven hour train ride from Milan. They told me to go, because if they liked me, they would use me. I went down there and it took forever to get a cab to take me to where GQ was, outside the city, which was another hour and a half ride. Barry McKinley, the photographer, was there and he had only seen one horrible picture of me. He liked me and decided to use me. Everyone was great and things worked out very well. I owe those people a lot. Out of sixteen pages shot, thirteen of them were mine, plus the cover.

The pictures weren't due to come out until September and this was only May, so I took the Polaroids from the shoot

Tom Tripodi's composite.

and I cut them out and put them in my book. When people saw those, I was booked a lot more. I started to work every day on the strength of being photographed by Barry McKinley for GQ. I stayed for three and a half months. But it was still difficult. I didn't even know how to comb my hair. If I had a hair dresser it was fine, but when I didn't the pictures were not as good. I wasn't very educated in the process yet.

When I returned to New York, I had my choice of going with either Ford or Zoli, and I was undecided. Barry McKinley favored Zoli, so I went with them. They've been great, and I've been with them for over six years now. When I started, most models were very all-American, and with my looks I was a little bit of a risk. Fortunately, a few years before I started, Thom Fleming and Jeff Aquilon had started the "jock look" so that helped me. Now, all types of people can be models, so it's a little easier for people to get into the business than when I started. Things have worked out fine, and it helped that I had a good business sense. Modeling is a business, and I made sure that I invested my earnings wisely for the future. The models who do very well today are very well educated, if not academically, then street-wise. Modeling is great, but the next step is commercials if you are looking for financial security. That took me a couple of years to discover, but when I did, I went after it. It took another couple of years of really trying to get into it. I found that I could make in one day what print modeling paid in several months. It's a natural progression, but it is almost like starting over. The doors may open a little faster when you're a top print model, but they'll close all the more quickly if you're not prepared.

The hardest part of keeping your career going is to continually do editorial to stay fresh. That keeps up your momentum. You may be making up to fifteen or twenty thousand dollars a month, but you need those editorial tears to insure that. It's tough to take the time out from making that kind of money to do the low-paying editorial work, but you must if you want to stay on top and remain fresh. Alternately, commercials will keep you fresh for clients, but if you aren't doing them, editorial is a must.

Eventually I'd like to do more legit work like film. Ten years from now I'd like to be up on the wide screen doing something good. That would be my idea of what should happen. But I have a degree in marketing and I love business; it comes naturally to me. Some friends of mine and I have started a business called Beastie Bags which are paper bag masks that kids can color and cut out and put on. They come in a portfolio with crayons, and so far it looks very promising.

I would never suggest that someone not go to school. It's important for the business. If you do really well, you can last a long time, but if you do mediocre, you can last maybe five years. If you last only five years, you can't make enough money to live on for the rest of your life. You need to have other options. If I was to set up a plan for someone, I would have them take all the courses they can, and if they're interested in acting, they should take a class in auditioning, and a commercial class. You've got to work at it and always be ready for what's going to happen. It's easier if you get breaks, but you can make a lot of your own breaks. You don't need to rush into things, take the time to enjoy yourself. If you go over to Europe, see the sights when you're not working. You have a marvelous opportunity to do that. I started modeling when I was twenty-six, and the business gets better as I get older.

PHOTO BY FRANCESCO SCAVULLO

A. J. Vincent

A. J. Vincent

I arrived in New York after leaving college with a degree in acting. I was twenty-two years old at the time. The first two or three theatrical agents who interviewed me asked me if I was a model. When I said no, they told me I should look into it. That's as far as I got with those agents at the time, but they did put the idea of modeling into my head. I started to think about it as a way to make money in a related field. To get started, I sought out some photographers and asked around about modeling agencies. I had test photos taken that didn't cost much. They were done in a rather impressive looking studio and were the best pictures of me I ever had. I was very green at that time, and could have been taken advantage of financially.

With pictures in hand, I managed to get started with a small agency which said I would be earning $100,000.00 a year in no time. That prediction was premature. I did start working almost right away doing some print, but mostly showroom and fit modeling. The agency didn't handle many people so they were able to concentrate on a select few. Before long, I had regular clients but I was eager to meet people, make contacts and be visible. When the man who ran the agency told me the buildings in the upper twenties and thirties, from Fifth Avenue to Seventh Avenue, were mostly clothing manufactures or clothing showrooms I got an idea. I started knocking on doors. Every day I picked a couple of buildings and looked at the directory, and if I saw men's manufacturers listed I went to the office and asked to see the person who hired the models. I covered many buildings starting on the top floor and working my way down. If they wouldn't let me in, I'd leave a card under the door and if I couldn't get past the receptionist, I would leave one with her. I think my greatest accomplishment in those days was canvasing The Empire State Building which is 102 floors. It took a long time to finish but I got clients. A lot of showroom work resulted which, eventually, lead to catalogs, press kits and ads. People were very nice, I think it was because I caught them off guard. They didn't have a lot of models walk in off the street; it wasn't something that happened to them every day. I suppose they thought I was pretty enterprising.

After a while, I wanted the prestige that went along with a big agency. I gave up being a big fish and it proved to be a difficult time for me. I no longer got the individualized attention I had in the smaller agency. It was frustrating to suddenly have little specialized attention and I left after a short while for Sue Charney's Faces. Faces is a mid-size agency where I've been for the last three years. They are big enough to allow me to make a living, but small enough to care about my progress and development. I am now in the process of changing from a young men's market into the men's market. Faces is not only capable of helping me make that change, but is willing to handle me during this transition. A lot of agencies wouldn't because when you switch markets, you are basically starting over. For the past five or six years my clients have all been young men's manufacturers or retailers. Now I'm getting into a briefcase, suit & tie kind of look where there is much more work. That is why men have the longevity in modeling that women do not. For males, you can start modeling as a boy, and grow from there to young men's, men's, and even later the distinguished older gentleman.

Meanwhile, I've continued developing my acting career and my skills as an actor. This is equivalent to having two full-time jobs. Modeling is a forty hour per week profession and acting is a forty hour per week profession, if not more for either

A. J. Vincent's composite.

Height 6'1"   Size 40R-L   Shirt 15½-34
Waist 31   Inseam 33½   Shoes 10   Hair Brown
Eyes Brown   SAG/AFTRA/AEA
Available for Shows

FACES FACES
212-661-1515
TELEX 697-1585

GLAMOUR
HOMMES
Tel. 4723-7019

Media Artists Group
role model

or both. There is always more to do or learn in a creative field. Once I realized I was the "product," and the "commodity," the responsibilities and demands of both careers became more clear. Even if I don't have a paying job on a given day there is still work that can be done. Auditions and go-sees, testings, contacting former clients with a new composite, reading a magazine for photographers names, seeing a play that might have a role that I could be right for are all part of my work day. There is no such thing as a part-time actor or model in a major city. You cannot be a part-time professional. You are either a professional or a non-professional. You're either a working model or actor or a non-working model or actor. There's no inbetween. There are too many people in competition with you for you not to be devoted to what you are doing. You have to make it happen.

As for my future, I hope to enjoy the move into the men's market. I will continue modeling and perhaps be able to do more commercial print. There, I can use my acting training to play characters for the camera instead of moods. I also hope to keep my acting career on the steady path it has taken by studying and working to build my resume. The possibility that the demands of one career could preclude my giving full attention to the other does exist. If that happens, I will happily direct my energies where they are needed.

My advice to anyone starting in this business is to be aware of your reasons for choosing the modeling or acting fields. If you are looking for glamor, excitement and celebrity then you may not, as yet, understand the workings of the industry. Those things may come your way, and I do stress *may*, but they are by-products of hard work, long hours, disappointments and diligence.

PHOTO BY CARMEN SCHIAVONI

Renauld White

Renauld White

I got into the business with the encouragement of a designer friend of mine, who worked in New York. He told me that it would be a good way to make some money. I was unsure about that. My father had been approached to be a model many years before in Chicago and had turned down the opportunity as too risky a profession on which to raise a family.

I gave it some thought although I really wanted to pursue acting. I came to New York and worked at various jobs, waiting on tables, and working in a shop. I had a good time, but after a while I decided to give modeling a chance. I went to several agencies to get information and finally signed with one. After a while I met another agent socially who had, at that time, a small agency. That was Zoli. He invited me to join his agency, but I hesitated because I was with a big agency, and I wasn't sure that he could do as well with my career as my current agency. He convinced me that he was very serious, so I changed to his agency.

Zoli was a wonderful man, very charismatic, with a great sense of style. I liked that. I was very impressionable. Everyone needs role models throughout their lives, not only when they're young. Everyone needs to have someone to emulate. Zoli was that kind of person to me.

Zoli had great insights into the business, and excellent connections. His parties were the best, with famous people in every corner. Things changed when Zoli and his partner split and he moved out of the townhouse he was in and moved to the agency's present location on Fifty-sixth Street. Several years ago he passed away, and the agency has changed, no doubt about it. Of course, the business has also changed. When I began, the money was there, the styles were distinct, there was direction, color, and shape. The creativity was flowing, and people had big budgets for a shooting. It was a freer time. Money didn't seem to get into the way of creativity as it does now. There were many more shows then, the designers weren't playing safe. Now it's different. The climate of the country is different. People are very safe. Budgets are tighter.

It's still a fascinating industry. You certainly are exposed to so many things. You get to go to a great many places, and although you usually aren't in one spot too long, you can often extend your stay after a shooting, and take advantage of a country that you might not otherwise have the opportunity to visit. Meeting people is also great. Every day it changes; every day is a different set of circumstances. It can be very exciting. It's not like a nine to five job, where you work with the same people every day and always know what to expect.

All the while that I've been modeling I've been continuing my acting. I've always had something working, whether it was a class, a off-off Broadway show, an independent film, or some theatre piece somewhere around the city. I'm now on a soap opera, *The Guiding Light*, playing William, a part I've played for three years. Because I started out wanting an acting career, I would eventually like to have that take most of my time. I would still take a few select modeling bookings, but my dream is to work on Broadway.

If you are interested in this profession, come into it prepared to do something else. Many are called, but few are chosen. If you are in school, by all means get your education, because it's never too late to get into this business. Most college graduates, at age twenty-two, still look and photograph like they're nineteen. It's a good profession, an honorable profession. You can't make the kind of money in any other business that you can make in modeling if you hit. However, don't lose sight of where you came from, because you have to realize where you're going to go. So make the money, but don't think that it's always going to be there. Act accordingly; save some for the future and enjoy some.

Renauld White's composite.

ROTEM

Jason Workman

Jason Workman

I started modeling at eighteen in Louisville, Kentucky. A girl that I was seeing was a model at the time, and I went with her to the agency one day. When I looked at the guys who were there, I thought 'I can do this.' They tried to enroll me in their modeling school, but I said I couldn't afford to take any lessons. They enrolled me anyway on a scholarship. They taught me a lot about runway and what to do on a shoot; I got a lot out of it. I stayed with them for two years, but didn't work much, partly because I lived in Lexington which was an hour away from Louisville, and partly because I was devoting much of my time to school.

In college I was studying accounting and business, but I wasn't sure what I wanted to do. I loved singing, and I left college for six months to work at a theatre in Florida. I did a couple of shows and really enjoyed it. I went back to college the next semester and hated it. I did some Summer stock in Louisville, and then in the Fall I went to Elite in Chicago, who had seen me at my agency in Louisville. There I really got a good taste of what the business was really about. Everyone says it's very cut-throat, but it wasn't; I was just ignorant about a lot of things. I knew what to do when I got a job, but it was how to go about getting the job that was difficult. If you're a new face, you need to get out and see as many people as possible. The agency helped, but basically it was sink or swim. They wanted to see if you could do it on your own. I stayed for about six months before returning to Louisville for the Spring, and Summer stock. In the Fall I returned to Chicago, and repeated my pattern of returning home for six months, for a period of three years. Unfortunately, by doing this, people found me unreliable. They couldn't book me anytime they wanted to because I was gone for six months of the year. Even while I was there, I wasn't booked very much, so I felt I was wasting my time.

I decided to go back to the theatre, and traveled around for the next four years, doing shows and revues. The last thing I did was on a cruise ship for six months. It was beautiful but boring. The shows were great, but I felt I wasn't going anywhere. A friend convinced me to try my luck in New York. I thought, 'I can't go to New York. That's the big-time!' But, I thought that if you can fail in Chicago, why not New York?

When I arrived in New York, I sent out a mailer with my picture and resume to many agents. Included in my list was HV Models. I didn't know that they only represented models, at this point I was trying to get a theatrical agent. I went in to see them, and they wanted to represent me. I wasn't sure that modeling was for me, but I decided to try again. The first few months were spent on go-sees and testing. The book I had was stripped and they started from scratch. It wasn't cheap to do this, but it was a lot better with agency support than trying to do it on your own.

I started getting a little catalog work after a couple of months, but I was basically supporting myself by waiting on tables. Work started to pick up; I began to work three to four days per week, and I started to gain confidence. Some people think I'm too confident, but I feel like I fit in. I haven't been to Europe, and although it might help my career, I'll probably never know as I have no plans to go there.

I'm still pursuing my acting career while I'm modeling, and I have a theatrical agent to handle that. Juggling both careers isn't easy, but so far it's working out. My first love is singing, but at this point I'm making more money modeling. I've never been happier than my time here in New York.

For the future, I'd like to continue modeling and acting for as long as I can. Eventually, I know I'll have to chose between the two, and I know it'll be acting that wins out.

If you think modeling is for you, give yourself a reasonable amount of time to check it out. Be persistent as hell, and don't let anyone tell you that you can't do something.

Height 6'1" Size 40R Shirt 15½-34 Waist 32
Inseam 34 Shoes 12 Hair Blonde Eyes Blue

Jason Workman's composite.

SECTION THREE

RESOURCES

RESOURCES

STORES

Model's Mart
17 East 48th Street
Sixth Floor
New York, NY 10017
(212) 688-7940
(800) 223-1254 (toll-free outside of New York)

Model's Mart carries most modeling books that are available, along with portfolios, video tapes, and mailing labels. You may visit them while in New York or order by telephone. They are very knowledgeable and helpful.

PORTFOLIOS

Model's portfolios come in many different sizes and shapes. Model's Mart (listed above) carries a good selection. You should also be able to find them at any good art supply store.

MINI BOOKS

The mini book is a small portfolio that is gaining favor. Basically it is just a smaller version of your big portfolio. Most any photographic service can reduce your tests and tearsheets to the proper size. We can recommend one excellent service, who handle orders from all over the country:

Bookitt
3333 Elm Street
Suite 103
Dallas, Texas 75226-9990
(214) 939-0105

COMPOSITES

All models have composites (also called "comps" or "cards"). These can be made at virtually any printer, but many places specialize in them. We can recommend four, although there are many more good ones:

Fleetwood Fashion Group
New York
(212) 886-2248

Peter Marlowe
New York
(212) 529-6666

Supershots
Los Angeles
(213) 724-4809

RESOURCES

187

Walkerprint International
New York
(212) 431-1121

Los Angeles
(213) 278-3847

London
01-580-7031

ORGANIZATIONS

The following group was formed to provide models with spiritual support and fulfillment. They have many activites and social events.

Models For Christ
P. O. Box 1109
New York, NY 10113
(212) 873-2133

GLOSSARY

AEA: Actor's Equity Association. A performer's union that encompasses most stage productions, especially Broadway.

AFTRA: American Federation of Television and Radio Artists. A performers union.

AD: An abbreviation of the word "advertisement."

AGENT: The person or company who represents a model or actor and gets him assignments.

ART DIRECTOR: The person from the advertising agency who is responsible for the design of an ad, and will probably be present at a shooting.

BEAUTY SHOT: Usually a close-up of the face, like you see on the cover of a magazine.

BODY SHOT: A photograph that shows your body to its best advantage, most often in a bathing suit, or at least without a shirt.

BOOK: When used as a noun, "book" means portfolio. When used as a verb, "book" is the act of reserving time on a model.

BOOK OUT: To set aside time that a model is not available for assignments.

BOOKER: The person at the modeling agency who takes appointments for the models and negotiates their fees.

BOOKING: A job.

CATTLE CALL: An audition or go-see where there will be a great many other models.

CHROME: A color transparency or "slide" that may be any size from 35mm to 8 X 10, and is a positive image.

CLIENT: The person or company who is hiring the model. This could be an art director, editor, owner of a company, etc.

COMMISSION: The percentage of a model's fee that is retained by a modeling agency as their share for services rendered.

COMPOSITE: A card that contains one or more pictures of a model that is left behind with a client on a go-see. Also called a "modeling card," "comp" or just a "card."

CONFIRMED: A definite booking.

CONTACT SHEET: A photographic print that contains a positive image of all the pictures from a roll of film, usually in black & white. These pictures are generally quite small (the same size as the negative) and are used to identify the different shots that were taken. You will use the contact sheet to select the photos you would like blown up for your card or portfolio. Also called a "proof sheet."

CYC: A wall that is used as a background for photography that is white, usually with a smooth curve merging the floor with the wall so there is no baseline visible and creates an "infinity" look.

DAY RATE: The fee a model receives for a full day booking.

EDITORIAL: Work that is done for a magazine or newspaper that is not for advertising purposes.

FLAT RATE: The fee a model will receive for a booking regardless of how long it takes to do.

GO-SEE: An appointment to see a prospective client.

HEAD SHOT: A close-up photograph of the face only.

HEADSHEET: A sheet or a book put out by a modeling agency containing photographs and statistics of the models they represent. These are sent by the agency to their clients.

LAYOUT: The design of a editorial or advertising page.

LOCATION: A shooting that either takes place outside of the photo studio or in a place outside of the city where the model is based.

MINI BOOK: A small portfolio (usually 5 X 7) that contains your tearsheets that have been photographically reduced to fit. This is very popular as it is easy to carry around and inexpensive to send out to clients.

MODEL RELEASE: A legal document signed by a model allowing photographs taken of him to be used in a certain way by the client. These should be read carefully before signing.

PLUS ONE: An extra hour of the model's time booked by a client that will only be paid for if used. Normally, every hour of a model's time that is booked must be paid for, even if the client is finished with the model early and lets him go.

PORTFOLIO: A case that contains a models photographs and tearsheets to show clients on go-sees.

PRINT WORK: Modeling work that is performed for still pictures that will appear "in print," such as in magazines or newspapers, either editorial or advertising.

ROUNDS: or "making the rounds" means going on appointments.

SAG: Screen Actor's Guild. A performer's union for movies and some television work.

SCALE: The minimum pay rate allowed by AFTRA, SAG or AEA. "Working for scale" means accepting the lowest possible fee.

SEAMLESS: The background on which a model is often shot, made of paper with no seams, that comes in many colors.

SHOOTING: A photography session.

SPREAD: Two or more pages devoted to one layout in a magazine.

STYLIST: The person responsible for the clothing, jewelry and props for a photography session.

TEARSHEET: The advertisement or editorial shooting that a model appears in, torn out of a magazine. These are used is a model's portfolio as examples of his work. Also called a "Tear."

TENTATIVE: A "hold" that is placed on the model's time, but is not yet a confirmed booking.

TEST: A shooting that is done to provide a model (or a photographer, makeup artist, etc.) with pictures that can be used in his portfolio but not for commercial purposes.

VOUCHER: A form that a model brings to a booking for the client to sign, confirming his hours spent there, and his rate. The model turns this into his agency to get paid.

WEATHER PERMIT: A booking that is outside that is booked on the condition that if the weather is bad, there will be no shooting that day.

FURTHER READING

FLASH! The Newsletter For Models.
 This eight-page newsletter is published six times per year and is full of helpful information for models. Subscriptions are $12.00. FLASH! 496 LaGuardia Place, Suite 145; New York, NY 10012.

The Insider's Guide To Modeling: The Pros Tell You How. By Eric Perkins. Nautilus Books 1985, $14.95.
 This hardcover book features interviews with top modeling professionals who tell you what they expect from a professional model.

International Directory of Model & Talent Agencies & Schools. Edited by David Vando. Peter Glenn Publications 1988, $25.00.
 This softcover book features the names and addresses of virtually every modeling agency and/or school in the United States, plus in many foreign countries. If you need to find the closest agency to you, this book is likely to have the information. A new edition is produced every year.

Male Model. By Charles Hix. St. Martin's Press 1979, $7.95.
 This softcover book is somewhat out of date, but still

provides interesting information. The best parts feature models talking about their careers.

NYC Model Agency Directory. Peter Glenn Publications 1987, $9.95.

This softcover directory lists New York agencies with their addresses and phone numbers, types of modeling the agency handles, basic physical requirements for each and more. A very handy guide for the beginning model.

Not Just Another Pretty Face. By Karen Hardy. The New American Library 1983, $11.95.

This softcover book is very interesting for it's interviews with twenty successful male models and many photographs.

Working Out: The Total Shape-up Guide For Men. By Charles Hix. Simon and Schuster 1983, $17.95.

This hardcover book (which is also available in softcover at a lower price) is a great book on exercise and grooming that is easy to follow and is profusely illustrated.

The World Of International Modeling. By Eve Matheson. Matheson Publications 1987, $12.95.

This softcover book is a helpful guide to modeling around the world. It not only lists the major modeling centers of the world, but it also names many of the top modeling agencies. The biggest plus is the city information, which describes the airports, public transportation, currency, banks, postal service, tourist information and more for each city. An invaluable guide if you plan to go to Europe.

AGENCY LIST

There are many agencies around the world that handle men and this list does not nearly list them all. Because many agencies come and go, you will always find new ones popping up and others falling by the wayside. This list only covers a few major cities, and some of the bigger agencies. If you would like to find a local agency, check your yellow pages telephone directory under the heading "Models." The listings below were correct as we went to press, however it is not unusual for agencies to change their locations or phone numbers, or even go out of business.

THE UNITED STATES

NEW YORK

New York City is the big-time, and is arguably the world's center of modeling. There are close to one hundred agencies in New York that handle models. Listed are some of the agencies that handle men.

Boss Models
321 West 13th Street
New York, NY 10014
(212) 242-2444

Click Models
881 Seventh Avenue
New York, NY 10019
(212) 315-2200

Elite Models
111 East 22nd Street
New York, NY 10010
(212) 529-9700

Faces (Sue Charney)
567 Third Avenue
New York, NY 10016
(212) 661-1515

Ford Models
344 East 59th Street
New York, NY 10022
(212) 838-2200

Foster-Fell
80 Varick Street
New York, NY 10013
(212) 226-4562

HV Models
18 East 53rd Street
New York, NY 10022
(212) 980-0793

Manner
874 Broadway
New York, NY 10003
(212) 475-5001

McDonald/Richards
156 Fifth Avenue
New York, NY 10010
(212) 627-3100

Men East
151 West 19th Street
New York, NY 10011
(212) 663-1990

Parts
Box 7529 FDR Station
New York, NY 10150
(212) 319-7249

Wilhelmina Models
9 East 37th Street
New York, NY 10016
(212) 532-7141

Zoli
146 East 56th Street
New York, NY 10022
(212) 758-6611

LOS ANGELES

Los Angeles is a big market, where the all-American look is very important. High fashion is usually not done here, but a great deal of commercial work, including catalog, is.

Nina Blanchard Agency
7060 Hollywood Boulevard
Suite 1010
Los Angeles, CA 90028
(213) 462-7274

Mary Webb Davis Agency
515 N. La Cienga Boulevard
Los Angeles, CA 90048
(213) 652-6850

Elite Models
9255 Sunset Boulevard
Los Angeles, CA 90069
(213) 274-9395

L.A. Models
8335 Sunset Boulevard
Los Angeles, CA 90069
(213) 656-9572

Smash Models
6725 Sunset Boulevard
Suite 506
Los Angeles, CA 90028
(213) 461-4060

Wilhelmina West
6430 Sunset Boulevard
Hollywood, CA 90028
(213) 464-4600

CHICAGO

Being a major city, there is quite a bit of work to be found in Chicago. There is a lot of good-paying catalog work done here, as well as just about every other kind of modeling. It is a good place for the beginning model to "learn the ropes."

Chicago Model Group
1445 N. State Parkway
Suite 28d
Chicago, IL 60610
(312) 944-3100

David & Lee Models
70 West Hubbard
Chicago, IL 60610
(312) 661-0500

Durkin Talent
743 N. LaSalle
Chicago, IL 60610
(312) 664-0037

Elite Models
212 West Superior
Suite 406
Chicago, IL 60611
(312) 943-3226

MIAMI

There is quite a lot of work in the Miami (and surrounding cities) area, especially (but not only) in the Winter months. Many Germans do location work here for their many catalogs. A model could make a very comfortable living here if he chose to.

L'Agence
8400 NW 52nd Street
Suite 227
Miami, FL 33166
(305) 255-7733

Irene Marie Agency
2400 E. Commercial Boulevard
Suite 430
Ft. Lauderdale, FL 33308
(305) 771-1400

INTERNATIONAL

PARIS, FRANCE

What can you say about Paris, that hasn't already been said? It's a city of fashion, romance, and incredible beauty.

There are many modeling opportunities, especially for editorial, fashion, and runway.

Bananas
217 Rue Du Faubourg
Saint-Honore
75008 Paris
4289-42-09

Best One
35 Rue Washington
75008 Paris
4225-24-12

Glamour
40 Rue Francoise 1
75008 Paris
4723-70-19

MILAN, ITALY

Milan is an important city for a new model as there is an enormous market, and tearsheets are not necessary to get started. There is plenty of magazine work and lots of runway. Most guys who head to Europe will end up here sooner or later.

Beatrice Models
Via Vicenzo Monti 47
20123 Milano
4988145

Fashion Model Service
6 Via Petrarca
20123 Milano
4986672

Why Not Uomo
Via Saffi 11
20123 Milano
4693831

LONDON, ENGLAND

A lot of work is to be had in London, although many guys never get there unless they are spending a long time in Europe. British Vogue, based in London, is one of the more prestigious magazines to work for.

Gavin's Models
11 Old Burlington Street
London W1
629-52-31

Model's One
Omega House
471-473 Kings Road
London SW10 OLU
351-60-33

Nev's Agency
36 Walpole Street
London SW3 4QS
730-06-15

INDEX

Don't miss our other fine titles!

The Insider's Guide To Modeling: The Pros Tell you How
Hardcover edition $14.95
Modeling advice from top professionals in the business.

Staying Thin: The Model's Health & Fitness Regimen
Hardcover edition $14.95
Get thin and stay healthy in this sensible diet and exercise plan.

The Staying Thin Cookbook
Hardcover edition $16.95
Over 150 delicious low calorie recipes to keep you looking great!

Staying Thin For Kids
Hardcover edition $16.95
A sensible health and fitness program for kids and their parents. Doctor approved.

The Broadway Celebrity Cookbook
Hardcover edition $19.95
Top Broadway Celebrities share their favorite recipes and food anecdotes. Available May 1989.

Available at fine bookstores everywhere or directly from the publisher.

Nautilus Books, Inc.
496 LaGuardia Place, Suite 145
New York, NY 10012